Testimonials

"Steve is a solo attorney and entrepreneur who has walked the walk and can show you exactly what you need to do, step by step, to achieve the success you truly deserve. You'll find Steve's no-nonsense approach to business to be extremely refreshing."

Dr. Tyson Franklin, DPM
Podiatry Business Consultant

"My good friend and longtime client Steve Richardson has exploded his solo law practice because he has very smartly created marketing processes that work really well by attracting, converting, and retaining only the best kinds of clients for his firm. The guy is a genius and can help any lawyer achieve the same and maybe even better success."

Tom Foster
Founder & CEO
Foster Web Marketing

"Steve Richardson is a very rare talent. He created and grew a true solo practice, from scratch. His years of building and enhancing that practice while providing real value and great service to his clients has given him an even rarer insight into what that takes and how to do it... day in and day out.

So whether you're looking for accountability for change and growth, strategic guidance, or new but proven tactics that work to build, market, or run a small or solo practice, Steve's knowledge and coaching might be exactly what you're searching for.

If you've been thinking about making changes and calming the chaos now may be the moment to take that first step. Call Steve."

David M. Frees, Esq.
Founder, Business Black Ops Marketing Mastermind Group

GETTING OFF THE HAMSTER WHEEL

Transforming Your Law Practice to Make More Money in Less Time Through Effective Systems and Marketing

STEVEN J. RICHARDSON, ESQ.

WORD ASSOCIATION PUBLISHERS
www.wordassociation.com
1.800.827.7903
TARENTUM, PENNSYLVANIA

Printed in the United States of America.

ISBN: 978-1-63385-439-0

Designed and published by
Word Association Publishers
205 Fifth Avenue
Tarentum, Pennsylvania 15084

www.wordassociation.com
1.800.827.7903

Introduction

However you came to be in possession of this book, I appreciate your getting a copy and opening it. I hope it does not disappoint. If you're anything like I was, you're feeling like your practice is spinning out of your control. You're working long hours (60+ hours, plus weekends), dealing with demanding, unreasonable clients, trying to get people to pay your bills on time so you have decent cash flow, and wasting time with tire-kicking potential clients or ones just looking for a free consult because they "just have a quick question." In short, your practice is controlling you, rather than the other way around.

This isn't what you envisioned when you went to law school. Whatever your reason was for becoming a lawyer, and however you envisioned the practice of law to be, reality has fallen far short of your expectations. Your law school professors taught you how to be a great lawyer and do the work of a law practice, but no one ever taught you how to run one. The truth is:

You are an entrepreneur, a law firm is a business, and you need to run it like one if you ever hope to be successful!

This is how my career went for many years. It certainly started out well. From high school on, I wanted to be a lawyer, so after graduating from Dickinson College in Pennsylvania, I went to law school at Rutgers University. After passing the bar in 1985, I worked for a few firms before getting the "entrepreneurial itch" and striking out on my own in 2000.

Because no one ever taught me how to do it, I did what everyone else did; I got an ad in the local phone book. That's what you did as a lawyer. But as a lifelong self-described "techno-geek" even then I knew I needed a website. I designed it myself using a product called Microsoft Front Page. It looked great, and I was one of the few lawyers in my area with a site and a custom domain - RichardsonLawOffices.com. The only problem was it didn't bring in any business!

For the next several years, I struggled to get high-quality clients with the phone book and an ad in a local newspaper, *The Shopper's Guide*. Cash flow was wildly unpredictable, and I never knew from one month to the next whether I would make a profit and be able to pay myself. I spent long hours at the office, because if I wasn't working **in** the business with enough cases, I had to work **on** the business to get more.

After a particularly abysmal month, I knew I had to go in a different direction if I was to survive. This led to my hiring a major legal marketing firm to do a new site for me after attending a seminar they put on in February of 2008. They overhauled it completely. It looked far more professional, had lots more content and, most importantly, it brought in business! I was making 2 to 3 times the cost of the site in new business!

But, in 2010, I came to the realization that I needed an even better website if I wanted to grow and do better. The one I had looked nice and was certainly bringing me business, but the more I wanted to do with it, the more I realized that my site couldn't handle it. I sat down with my account representative and gave him a list of what I wanted to do. Every time I asked him a question, I got a blank look or an additional cost that was way out of control.

I then started searching around for a new company that "got it," that understood where modern legal marketing was going online and could implement all of the things on my list with alacrity. I ultimately decided on a company in Fairfax, Virginia, Foster Web Marketing, that definitely "got it."

From my initial phone discussion with their sales representative, where we seemed to finish each other's sentences in discussing online projects, I knew they were the firm that could implement my plans. They also came highly recommended by a college friend of mine, Dave Frees, an estate planning lawyer in Pennsylvania, and a widely recognized business and marketing consultant and coach (I later joined his mastermind group, Business Black Ops). You will hear more about him later on in this book.

My site launched with Foster Web Marketing in August of that year, and I haven't looked back. That was also when I started to realize the enormity of the marketing job I had taken on. In addition to practicing law full time, I also had to write 2 to 3 pieces of content per week, upload one video a week, and design multiple e-mail campaigns to engage the leads that I attracted with my site. It was driving me crazy!

This is also not to mention the dozens of books and blog articles I read on marketing, podcasts I listened to, and other research I did to get the necessary marketing skills to make all of this work properly and effectively. It is an ongoing educational process, as there is always more to learn, so I keep reading and listening.

Problem was, although I was doing better, I still felt out of control and working long hours! I was going crazy!

So, to save my sanity, and make sure that my business grew and thrived, I started implementing automations, systems and procedures to get it all done. This, along with ruthless time management, has made it possible for me to do all of this and still have time for my wife, my friends, and my other interests.

Over the years, I have been asked, how do you get it all done? How do you find the time? The more I thought about it, the more I realized that I had to write it all down. In order to be able to answer those questions from friends and colleagues, I had to synthesize it and organize it into something that I could relate to others. I had to have a formalized system (more on that in the next section). That is the reason you are holding this book right now.

Buster Tate, the COO of Foster Web Marketing, once called what I do "The Richardson System." I guess it is just that, for lack of a better term. So, in this book I hope to explain that system and, more importantly, pass it on to you, so that you don't have to go through what I did to get where I am. Bear in mind, though, that my system is mine and works for me; it might not work for you in every instance, but it should make for a good guide.

Also, although I chose FWM to design and host my site, you do not have to in order to benefit from the ideas and techniques in this book. However, if you do realize from what I discuss that your current provider doesn't have the capabilities you need (like I did in 2010), I would certainly suggest that you check them out. They offer a free website analysis that will get you started.

Chapter One

Making the Time

Time Management

You can read this book in any order you like, but if you are ever going to succeed in transforming your law practice into a business, you should really start with how you view your time. As I said in the introduction, one of the most frequent questions I am asked is: How do you find the time? The answer can be found in this chapter, and I would suggest to you that you need to **find** that time before you can **use it** effectively in your business or practice and implement The Richardson System. So start here and follow along.

Time is Finite

This is huge. The people that say that "time is money" have it wrong. They are not equal; they are very different. If I spend $100 of my money on something and it doesn't work out, I can just work harder the next day to make that money back and then some! But if I lose an hour, I will never get it back! Also, where money is somewhat infinite, time is not. It is finite. Everyone gets just 24 hours in a day. How you spend it is up to you, but if you waste it, you will never get it back!

Time is therefore your most precious commodity, and you must guard it jealously! It is yours, and never let anyone take it from you without your consent — and grant that consent judiciously. Be tough; be ruthless. It is your time, it is your life, and no one has the right to take it from you or force you to use it in a particular way. If you don't take charge of your time, you will never have enough of it.

The Time Bandits

There was a movie that came out in 1981 called *Time Bandits*. It was very funny and I loved it when I saw it, but I am going to steal the title here to make a point. There are time bandits in your life, and they are going to try and steal your time. Don't let them! These time bandits come in many forms, and not all of them are evil or malicious. Many of them will be your friends, family, and longtime colleagues. But that doesn't mean that they aren't a serious threat to you! You must beware of them, nonetheless. The most insidious of all of them, though, is . . .

Mr. "Got a Minute"

I hate this guy! He has stolen so much of my time over the years and has to be one of the biggest time bandits of them all! I am sure you recognize him just from his name and the damage he can do to your day. You are hard at work on something, you are "in the zone," getting things done, and you hear a knock at your office door. He stands on the threshold, grinning, and wants to talk to you about something.

You can ignore him, but he is a persistent SOB, and he won't go away! He will just stand there until you acknowledge him, and when you do, he will ask, "Hey, have you got a minute?" What you say next is critical because guess what? It's never just a minute! It's at least 15 to 20 of them, and he seldom wants to talk about anything that will help you.

He may have a problem that he wants you to solve for him, but often he just wants to blather on about how the Eagles did against the Cowboys in last night's game! Before you know it, you've lost half an hour, haven't completed the task you were working on, have fallen out of the "zone," and realized that you have a client meeting in 5 minutes, so you can't get back to it!

This Time Bandit is telling you that your time is less valuable than his, that whatever you are doing is unimportant and is easily interrupted. Here's what you said to him in response:

"I'm busy right now. Let's meet at 4pm for 15 minutes and tackle everything on your list at one time."

This will stop him in his tracks, but you may need to do it more than once for him to get the message. Eventually he will.

The Drama Queen

These time bandits have the ability to turn even the smallest thing into a big deal that will take 20 to 30 minutes (or more) to talk to you about. They will turn that molehill into a mountain. If you have a colleague in your office or support staff that is a drama queen, then you need to drive them away. Dan Kennedy, in his book *No B.S. Time Management for Entrepreneurs*,[1] suggests two ways to do this:

Interrupt them, force them to come to the core of the topic and tell them what to do. This will frustrate their efforts to bring drama into it and talk for hours.

Turn the tables on them and take over the conversation by being an even bigger drama queen. This will take the focus and attention off them, which is what they really want, and they will go away.

1. Which I highly recommend you read from cover to cover.

We'd Love It If You Would . . .

This time bandit can be very hard to fend off. They want you to do something for them (or their organization) and, no matter the size of the commitment, it will steal your time. Maybe it's running a fundraiser for the Rotary or Lion's Club or coaching your son's soccer team. It is often something that, at some level, you do want to do. However, as time is finite, whatever time it takes from you has an "opportunity cost." If you do that thing, you will not be able to do something else with that time.

My friend Dave Frees, whom I mentioned earlier, has a way of dealing with these time bandits. He provides a simple test to gauge your answer. In short, "If it isn't a hell yeah, it's a no." Is it something you've always wanted to do? Something that, when asked to do it, you want to just jump up and kiss the person that asked you? Will it not take time away from something else that is more in alignment with your purpose, goals, or mission? If so, then yes, do it. It's a good use of your time. If not, just say no.

But be nice about it. Remember, it's "Hell yeah," not "Hell no!" Dave typically says to the person, "Thank you for asking me! I am honored that you thought I would be the perfect person to do this. However, with the projects I am currently committed to, I would not have the time that would be sufficient to do the quality job we would both want me to do, and I would ultimately be doing you a disservice by saying yes. For that reason, I must say no." In this way you are not turning them down, you are trying to help them by saying that you are not the right person for the job.

Those Pesky Clients & Potential Clients!

One of the toughest things you are going to have to do in order to regain, and maintain, control of your time is to manage the client and potential client time bandit. This means **do not make or take ANY unscheduled calls!**[2] If you take inbound calls as they come, you are constantly stopping work on a task of known priority in favor of something or someone of unknown priority. You are turning control of your day over to the unknown.

I know, I know, this is easier said than done, but it must be done. Every time you take an unscheduled call, no matter who it's from, you are disrupting your focus on the work you are doing. You lose time not only due to the phone call, but also in the time it will take you to regain focus after you hang up!

Many of my colleagues have the fear that if they don't answer the phone and talk to them right away, the prospective client will then just call someone else or the client will get angry and fire them. Dan Kennedy's response to this is, "if you are that interchangeable, that mundane and ordinary a commodity, you've got big, big problems, far bigger than you can solve by answering your phone immediately."

I will discuss later in this book ways of implementing this policy, but there are things you will need to do first to make the rest possible. Regarding clients, you need to manage their expectations from the very start. Explain to them that in order to give them the best representation possible, you want to be able to work on their matters uninterrupted. Say that

2. There are exceptions, of course, which I will discuss in detail.

you're sure that they wouldn't want you to drop what you are doing on their file in order to take a call from another client, so the reverse would have to be true in order to prevent that from happening.

At the same time, assure them that you are always happy to discuss their case with them if they have any questions or want a status update. They just have to schedule a call. Put it in your engagement letter and discuss it with them at the retention meeting, so that they know from the very start.

Then there are the potential clients. When a lead calls, you may be tempted to stop what you're doing and take the call. After all, this could be the next big case! But again, this is a time bandit. You can't risk the loss of focus or time that answering would cause. You therefore need a dedicated intake person to talk with them initially. Have them take the initial information, and then, if it is worth your time to meet with them, according to criteria you provide to your intake person, then he or she can schedule an appointment for them to come in to meet with you. This will again keep you focused and eliminate another type of interruption. The added bonus will be to set expectations with that person at the very beginning that they just can't call and expect to be put through to you.

I am not saying that there aren't any exceptions to this, however. If a judge's chamber is calling, you take the call! If it is a client calling with a (true) emergency, you take the call! If it is your spouse to tell you your child was injured, you take the call! However, your secretary/assistant should always be the gatekeeper. If it is something he or she can easily handle (or handle with some quick input from you) then great. You don't have to take the call and lose your focus; you have people for that!

If you are worried about missing the truly important call, provide your secretary or receptionist with a "VIP list" of people from whom you will almost always take an incoming call, regardless of what else you may be doing. This will prevent you from missing calls that you really want and allows your assistant to screen all the other calls with greater confidence.

Control the time on VIP list calls, though. When you get on the phone with the VIP, always set up an exit time right away. For example, "I have another call starting in 15 minutes, but I wanted to take your call. I hope that will be enough time for our discussion. Do you agree, or should we set up another telephone appointment?"

This can be done as well with people that drop into your office, assuming you even tolerate walk-ins. Say something like, "It's difficult these days for me to see drop in visitors, but it's good to see you. I will only have (set time frame here), but no longer, as I have an important conference call set for (set time here). That's OK, isn't it?"

This not only helps you to assert control over your time, it also helps train people to set up a phone appointment or a time to meet with you personally that fits into your calendar.

And Then There's E-Mail!

This has to be one of the biggest time bandits of them all! So many attorneys and professionals I know talk about checking their e-mail first thing in the morning. **Don't do it!** Once you go to your Inbox, it can be very difficult to get out. You may say to yourself that you will only check for 5 minutes, but you later look up at the clock and see that it's been 45! Also, if you have alerts set on your computer for when an e-mail comes in, turn them off. Even if you aren't in your Inbox, if you're working on a client project and that alert comes in, it's a distraction. You stop what you're doing and look at what just came in.

What is the Richardson System? I check my e-mail after lunch, and again at the end of the day. That's it! I let my clients know that that's how I handle it, so that they know that if they send me a message in the evening, I won't see it until the following afternoon. I check after lunch to see if there are any urgent matters I need to address. I check at the end of the day to see what I have to do for the following day (as you will see later in this book, I plan the next day just before I leave the office from the current one).

And the Dreaded Meeting!

Depending on the size of your firm, and how much staff you have, getting sucked into meetings can also be a big-time bandit! These meetings are never productive and seldom accomplish anything. When Mr. Meeting tries to steal your time, ask yourself: is there a more efficient way to handle this? Can we do a quick conference call? Anything is better than a meeting! Some other ideas are:

- Schedule the meeting for you to leave before lunch or at the end of the day, so that people will be motivated to finish up and move on
- Don't serve refreshments
- Insist that a written agenda be submitted in advance and circulated to all attendees
- Have and communicate a clear, achievable objective for the meeting

pad. Remove your phone; you aren't going to be taking or making any phone calls during this process, so there's no use having it. Then when you have a clear workspace and the necessary tools, you are ready to begin.

Gathering the Tasks

A good start would be with your files and legal work. Pull every file out of your cabinets, or work through them drawer by drawer. Go through each file and make a list on a page of the legal pad of everything that needs to be done on that matter. Go through any unfiled documents, such as incoming correspondence, to make sure that you don't miss anything. On the computer, go through every e-mail in your inbox and make a list of them (or print them out and make a stack of them in the in-box).

After that, go through anything else in your office (as well as the desks of your staff) and sift through it in the same way. Wrack your brain of everything that has been rattling around in it that needs to be done and write them down on the legal pad. Once your legal pad is filled, you need to create your Trusted System to put it all in for processing.

Processing the Tasks

Once you have gathered all your tasks together, you have a baseline of work to do. Naturally, the process of gathering Tasks and Projects[4] is ongoing, so you need a system for capturing tasks into your Trusted System as they occur to you. But once everything is gathered, you need to process it by following the 4 Ds: Do It, Defer It, Delegate It, Dump it.

4. See below for the distinction.

The first determination is, is it actionable? Do you need to do anything with that document, e-mail, phone message? Do you need to keep it for some reason? If not, then Dump It. If you need it for future reference, though, then file it away in a separate database/trusted system. If you think you might want to act on it someday, put it in a Someday folder.

If it is actionable, does it have one step or several? If the latter, it is a Project, and you need to break it down into its component Tasks first (see Tasks v. Projects below). Then, with each Task:

- Can it be done in less than 2 minutes? If so, then Do It right now
- If more than 2 minutes, then
    - If you must do it, Defer It to a future time on your calendar
    - If someone else can do it, Delegate It to a staff member (and diary a follow-up with that staff person)

Your Trusted System

How you set up and implement your Trusted System is up to you. There is no right or wrong way to do it, as long as it meets the goals and requirements of David Allen's GTD system. The most important criterion is: Is it something you will stick to? Is it something you will actually use?

You can use paper and folders, but as I said before, I think a paperless, electronic system is best. There are many task management programs out there, and which one you choose is up to you and the computing platform you use. However, I believe that to work well, they need to have these capabilities and features:

- The ability to review all your tasks and p periodically. I do this every Sunday morning. Thi: to having control over your work.
- The ability to capture Tasks and Projects as they o you. My system has a hotkey I can press to add son on the fly to review later. I can also dictate it throu
- The ability to distinguish between Tasks and Proj you can properly break down and organize your w

The first two capabilities are key. I cannot stress enou importance of having a method to capture Tasks and P The best time to get something into your system is the n you think of it. Thus, you will be far less likely to forge it, and you will be relieved of the stress of worrying might not get done. The Task or Project is in your System! Failing to do this creates frustration and stres remember at the end of the day that I need to do son that isn't on the list! Thus, the task remains undone, a stress continues until it gets into my system

The second thing is to plan a review of all your Projects Sunday morning, I review all of my Projects and Task: what needs to be done in the coming week. This give sense of control over my work and helps me to decid to take on in the next 5 days. I include matters that I address both **in** and **on** my business. It also prods my b think of things that need to be added to projects that I thought of before, or that had been rattling around back of my brain.

I work in the Apple Ecosystem, so my Trusted Syster app called OmniFocus. It works on my Mac and my tablet, thus allowing me to wrangle my Tasks and P

no matter where I am. But there are many others, including Things, Todoist, Outlook Tasks, and Microsoft Todo. Just pick one and stick with it!

Tasks v. Projects: Understanding the Distinction

The difference between a Task and a Project is important. Understanding the distinction can transform how you look at, and approach, your work. A Task is an item of work that contains a single step. If you look at a Task and realize that there are several things that need to be done to accomplish it, it is really a Project.

For example, let's say your spouse asks you to do the food shopping for the week. But before you get into your car to go to the supermarket, consider the steps that really need to be taken:

- Make a list of meals for the week
- Look up the recipes for those meals to check the ingredients
- Check the pantry to see what items you have and what items you need
- Make a shopping list of those items you need
- Go to the store and buy the items on the list
- Put away the food once you get home

Seeing all of the steps involved and distinguishing between a Task and a Project allows you to plan out your day much better and estimate the time that needs to be set aside to accomplish it.

Now apply that to something in your professional life. You have a trial coming up in a couple of weeks and you need to prepare. Well, under this analysis, "Prepare for Trial" is not a Task; it's a Project. So let's break it down. You need to:

- Organize exhibits
- Prepare Direct Examination of Witness X (a separate task for each witness)
- Prepare Cross Examination of Witness Y (each one)
- Prepare Opening Statement
- Serve subpoenas on third party witnesses (which can break down to)
    - Prepare Subpoena
    - Arrange for Process Server
- Secure Proof of Service
- Meet with and Prep Client
- Meet with and Prep Witness Z (each one)
- Prepare Closing Statement

As you can see, this breaks down into many different Tasks.

The advantage here is that you can break down the Project and plan the Tasks for the various days leading up to the trial. This allows you to execute the project methodically, in the proper order of priority, and to view it in smaller, more achievable pieces, rather than this massive overall thing you have to do. You are also focusing on the task in front of you, and the time it will take to accomplish, rather than be overwhelmed by the overall Project (which only creates more stress).

You can also decide for each one whether it is something you need to do or something you can delegate. So when you are planning your week, you can distribute the Tasks over those 40 hours (and hopefully not too many more, if you have true dominion over your time). This concept also applies to working **on** your business, as well as in it. By having dominion over your time and control over your work, you can structure your workdays with the various Tasks that have the most priority in your practice.

Finding Your One Thing

Gary Keller, owner of Keller/Williams Realty, talks about finding your One Thing every day. Ask yourself, "What is the one thing I can do, such that by doing it, everything else will be easier or unnecessary?" By determining the answer to this question every morning (or every evening as you plan the next day), you are gaining the focus that is necessary to be the most efficient and effective you can be.

I recommend doing this on Sunday evening (to plan your week) or every evening to plan the next day. Go through all of your Projects and their most high priority tasks and find the Number One thing you need to do next that will meet Keller's definition. You can stick to one task, but if you need to do more in a day, I recommend you choose a maximum of three.

If you are able to accomplish everything for that day with time left over, great! But if you look up from your desk and see that it is after 5pm, you at least know that your time was spent on the most important things you needed to accomplish. You may also have saved some time on other downstream tasks that have become easier or unnecessary due to your following this plan.

Time Blocking

Now that you have dominion over your time and control over your work, the next step is to plan out your time. This is often referred to as block scheduling or time blocking. You may have a list of things you want to do tomorrow, but if you don't have a clear idea of how much time it will take you to do it, you can end up spinning your wheels.

You are basically making an appointment with yourself to work on a particular task or project. In doing this, you have to have integrity and keep your word. What do I mean by that? I mean that you have to show up on time to that appointment. Whatever you are doing at the time has to stop, so that you can move on to your next appointment. If you do not do this, then the current task will eat into the time for the next one, and that successor task may never get done.

Mapping Out Your Day

This time blocking can be done on a daily, weekly, monthly, and annual basis. It all depends upon how long range your projects are. If you know you have a trial coming up next month, block out time in the intervening weeks to prepare for it. This will prevent it from being filled up by other things (client meetings, initial consultations) that can distract you and take time away from this high priority project.

Are you planning a vacation? Block out the time now, even if it's 6 months away. Want to have a few "mental health days" scattered throughout the year? Put them on your calendar now, so that day off has "dibs," and you will be forced to plan around it to preserve that time. The important thing is to think beyond the next day in the office. Be more strategic in your time blocking and use that evening before to tweak the schedule a bit and fill in the gaps.

Daily Time Blocking

In planning your tomorrow, look at the 1 to 3 things you have planned to do, and then do your best to estimate the amount of time each task will take (then round up). Always assume it will take longer than you think it will. Set alerts on your electronic calendar for five, 10, and 15 minutes before each time block, to help me remember to wrap up the task you're working on, in order to be ready to move onto the next.

> *Dan Kennedy and other business coaches recommend setting aside one day a week as your "marketing day."*

In my office, each workday has three standard tasks that I schedule for 30-minute slots. From 9 to 9:30 AM, I return calls from the previous day. From 1:30 to 2 PM, I review my email inbox. From 4:30 to 5 PM, I review emails again and block my time for the following day, to the extent they are not already commitments on my calendar. Then I fill in my time from there.

During the time blocked, be rigorously focused. Do not be tempted to do other things, such as checking email or other time-wasting activities. Then when that time block ends, wrap up what you are doing and move on to the next task.

The idea is to leverage unproductive time during your workday. Stuck in the waiting room of your doctor's office? Be sure to bring with you a tablet or e-reader and get some reading done. I have an iPad and Apple Pencil and use them to review documents electronically. I can just pull that out of my bag and get that done in time that would otherwise have been unproductive and make me expend more time outside of the workday to make up for it.

One of the things I do to capture odds and ends of time is have items on my to-do list that do not have a specific date to accomplish, but also don't take a lot of time to do. I tag them in my system as "quickies." If I finish a task early, I will pull up my Quickies List and see what I can accomplish in the spare time before the next task is scheduled to begin. Try it!

How I Can Help

I know I have thrown a lot at you and that accomplishing all of this is easier said than done. It is going to take time (ironically enough) and effort to accomplish, but you will be glad you did once your systems are in place. Also, every practice is different, and molding some of the concepts to yours takes some thought. Fortunately, you are not alone in this.

If you need help with getting dominion and control over your time and work, I do offer coaching and consulting services designed to get you to where you need to be. Feel free to reach out to me through my web site at www.StevenJRichardson.com to get a conversation going. You can also look at the Resources listed at the end of this book for more help.

Automation

Now that you've established dominion over your time and control of your work, you can then move on to the final stage of the time management process: Doing more of that work in less time! As I stated earlier, systems create efficiencies that save time and allow you to do a better and more consistent job. Automation plays a big part.

There are a lot of repetitive tasks that take up a lawyer's day. What if you could find a way to do them faster? What if you had a number of routine letters to send out that could be done in a matter of minutes instead of an hour? That's where automation comes in. There are many ways to accomplish this, which I will discuss in the sections that follow. But just like time management, automation takes a mindset and is part of system-building. However, that mindset is easier to convey and comes in just two parts. Every time you set out to do a task, ask yourself one of these two questions:

- How can I automate this?
- How did I automate this?

Like most everything else I discuss in this book, automation is something that is going to take an investment of time. But just like an investment of money, your time will grow way past the initial investment (if done well). The task you automate will take longer to do the first time, because you are not just doing it, you are creating the automation, but the time saved later will more than make up for it.

For example, let's say it takes you an hour to automate a task that would take you 30 minutes to do otherwise. But with the automation, that task will now take 10 minutes. You are investing 30 minutes which you will get back after doing that task twice more. After that, you will have an extra 20 minutes available to you to do something else.

Yes, you probably know that without my having to tell you, but I hope that my explanation reinforces the importance of the investment. It should also make clearer to you that there is actually a third question that should be in your mindset: **Should** I automate this?

But what does that mean? Well, how often do you do this task? Is it on a regular basis or every once in a while? How long would it take for the investment of time to pay off for you? When would you start **saving** time and stop **regaining** time? For automation to be effective, this third question should also be asked.

Automation should also be downstream. Your staff (if you have any) should also be working to automate what they do, and this is accomplished through the systems you establish for their workflow. You are investing **money** for their **time**, and the more they are able to do for the same money will also pay off for you handsomely. Are you thinking of hiring your first staff person because you are overloaded with things to do? What if the time you save through automation allowed you to defer the hiring of someone (and save the money you would have spent on salary and benefits)? What if you have a staff person, but need to hire another to take on an additional load as you expand? By automating staff tasks, you could save money or at least defer spending it on that hire!

There are many different tasks that can be automated, and therefore different ways to automate them. There are also different **ways** to **think** about automation. Therefore, in this section, I am going to talk about each of these types of tasks and what kinds of automation can be brought to bear to automate them

However, because hardware and software can differ (I use Macs and other Apple products in my practice), along with types of practices, I cannot get into a lot of specifics on how to automate the tasks. How I may automate things might not help you if you have a Windows system.

What I will do is give examples, and suggest certain products, so that you will have a better idea of how to get started. I also have a section for Apple users that talks about automation tools available on that platform. Should you need more guidance, please e-mail me at steve@stevenjrichardson.com or contact me through my web site at www.StevenJRichardson.com to determine your needs and see if one of my coaching programs would help you.

Automation Features in Apps

One of the great things about automation is that you can start doing it without spending any extra money. There are lots of apps and utilities for automation, which I will discuss later in this book, but there are a lot of things you can do now with the programs you already have in order to save a lot of time in your practice, time that could be put to better, more profitable uses. If you are just getting your feet wet with automation, I would start with these.

E-Mail (Outlook)

We all get a ton of email, and more floo
But getting to inbox zero can be hard and
Luckily, apps like Outlook and Apple Mail ha
function called Rules that are often underu
However, implementing them can certainly
time. I will use Outlook 365 as an example, si
the program you are using, but these princip
rules feature of most email programs.

Focused View

But before I get into that, I want to talk about
that Outlook has called the Focused view. Wh
was released, I started using it immediately an
definitely enhanced my ability to focus on wh
my email communications. As emails come in
program assigns it to either the Focused view
view. It worked fairly well from the start, se
my case related emails from the junk I receive.
much easier for me to get to Inbox Zero becaus
with fewer emails in my Focused inbox.

As you continue to use it, you can help it al
clicking on an email and then telling it to mov
the focused view from other or the other view fi
either just that one time or always. After a while,
gets pretty good at it. I would recommend you tu
soon as you can. In fact, put this book down and

Rules

ıles govern what happens to an email once it comes into your stem. Beyond relegating an email to the Other view, Outlook d other email apps can process incoming email based on les and criteria that you create. In the Windows version, ick on the File menu, then on the Account Information ige, select Rules and Alerts. On the Mac version, go to the ools menu and select the Rules option. Both methods will ring up a dialog box listing all your rules and giving you n opportunity to create new ones. However, the Windows ersion currently offers you some "canned" rules as templates nat you can tweak to get the idea.

n general, an email rule is in two parts. The first part is the lter, and the second part is the action. In the filter, you are etting forth what criteria an incoming email must meet n order for the designated action to be taken. Those filters an look at who the messages are from, the subject line, the ody of the message, the date it was received, whether or ıot it has attachments, or the kind of message it is (whether t is encrypted, an email automatically forwarded to you, a meeting request, a meeting response, or a read receipt). Not only that, but it can search for more than one. So, for example, you can say that if the message is from John Smith and it is marked urgent, then take the following action.

If a message is found to have met the criteria, then the rule can take one or more actions on that message. It can move or copy it to another folder, automatically mark it as read, prioritize it in some way (low, normal, or high), or categorize it. You can also add an extra layer called "except if." This allows you to get even more granular with your rules.

Let's say you keep a separate folder in Outlook for each of the matters you are handling. You can create rules that will take emails from that client and automatically move it to that client's folder. A rule can also help you to cull through a lot of emails you do not need to read or keep by deleting them or moving them to a "Review Later" folder. The more you explore the rules options, the more ideas will come to mind. You will soon be the master of your inbox!

Case Management Software (Document Automation)

A lot of great opportunities for automation can be found in your case management software. Now I use Clio, but when I was deciding on a case management platform, I saw that other vendors had these features as well. Therefore, I suspect you will find it in Rocket Matter, MyCase, Practice Panther, Filevine, and others. Although I will use automation in Clio as an example, I am sure you will find parallels in your software, if you are not a Clio user.

Clio helps maintain a paperless office. Compatible with my Fujitsu ScanSnap scanner,[5] I can touch a button to scan the document and trigger a dialog box on my computer screen that allows me to enter a name for the document, the matter it relates to, and what document folder it should go into. It then gets automatically saved to Clio. I can also download the document to my OneDrive folder through Clio's OneDrive integration.[6]

5. Which I have found to be the scanner of choice for lawyers.

6. Although Clio and other platforms also support Google Drive, Dropbox, and others.

Outgoing documents are also automated. Every time you create a document you should ask yourself, "Can I make a template from this?" This investment of additional time will definitely pay dividends down the road. Routine correspondence can be created and sent in a snap, along with retainer agreements, pleadings, discovery documents, and the like. The more you think about it, the more use cases you will find.

You should also give some thought to adding custom fields to your matter and contact entries. The more information about a case that you have in your system, the more information there is to be merged into your documents. Part of my practice involves doing criminal expungements. These petitions can be tedious to prepare, as there is a lot of specific information that needs to be plugged into the legal document. Once I created the necessary custom fields in Clio and put them into my expungement petition form, preparing the paperwork became a snap.

Your CRM Platform

Your contact relationship management (CRM) software also provides you with some terrific automation tools, which to a great extent is the whole purpose of having a CRM system. All sorts of automated actions can occur when triggered by the addition of a new contact. If the new contact subscribes to your email, then it is automatically added to the email list for the newsletter and starts receiving it. If the contact downloaded one of your offers or lead magnets, it can be automatically added to a drip campaign for that particular offer. Those emails then are sent out according to how that campaign was structured, without you having to do a thing. Some emails can even be sent out on a specific date, like a birthday or a wedding anniversary. It all depends on the features of your CRM software.

Further discussion about how your CRM software can automate your marketing and save you time is covered in the section on laying out a campaign. Just bear in mind and appreciate the fact that this software automates tasks that would take you hours to do by hand.

Automation Platforms

Automation platforms on your computer can save you a lot of time and money. They can do many repetitive tasks automatically and much faster than you can. They can reduce errors, because once you have it set up it will do the task the same way every time. Can you say the same for yourself if you did it manually? We are human, and prone to errors, but machines will do exactly what you tell them to do in exactly the way you tell them to do it. No matter the automation platform you use, if it works with your apps, there are all sorts of things you can do to save you time.

Unlike what I discussed in the previous section, these are not automation features in an app; these are apps that exist solely to create automations. It is these platforms that I will discuss here. Recognizing that most lawyers use Windows PCs, I will talk about 2 cloud-based automation platforms: Zapier and Microsoft Power Automate. Later, I will discuss how Mac users can leverage automation.

In a previous section where I talk about cloud platforms, I recommend Microsoft 365 for its holistic approach to cloud computing. One of the advantages of this platform is its integrated automation system. But if you are not using Microsoft 365, and have no plans to migrate to it, then Zapier is worth looking into.

General Concepts

These two platforms have common concepts that, once you master them, will make it easy to create automations no matter what system you use. The two basic concepts are: triggers and actions. Triggers are what cause automations to execute, and actions are what the automations actually do. As to triggers, they can be something that involved an affirmative action by you (such as hitting a particular keyboard combination), an event that occurs in a particular app, or an event that happens at a particular time. Apps that are compatible with Zapier have created triggers and actions within their applications, and you can use these building blocks to create automations.

For example, when my virtual assistant completes a task that I set for her in Microsoft To Do (the trigger), the system sends me an alert to tell me that she did it (the action). This helps me to supervise her work and know what's going on. In answering the question, "How can I automate this?" think about what the trigger would be in what application. Then see whether that trigger and application are available on your automation platform.

Zapier

Zapier is perhaps the best-known automation platform, and for good reason. Lots of applications are compatible with it and provide triggers and actions to create great automated

How many routine things happen in the course of your workday where a particular event leads to other tasks? The event is the trigger, and the task is the action. Think of the event in terms of the app in which it occurs, then see what actions are available for it in your automation program. This will help you answer the question: Can I automate this (and also, should you automate this)?

APPLE SHORTCUTS

Yes, I did state that I would discuss automation programs that could run on any system (Windows, Mac, etc.), as most lawyers use Windows. However, with the popularity of the iPhone and the domination of the iPad in the tablet market, I would be remiss if I did not discuss one other program: Apple Shortcuts. Although they are much more effective for users that also have Mac desktops and laptops, they can still be very powerful for those who have Windows computers and Apple portable devices.

Apple smartphones and tablets are compatible with all sorts of Microsoft applications and other Windows compatible programs because their developers have created an app for them. For example, there are all sorts of automations you can run on your calendar or your email. These changes then get synchronized with your PC. For example, as I said in the time management section, I do time blocking and plan my day the evening before. I also stated that I have 3 Standard Time blocks: one from 9:00 AM to 9:30 AM, one from 1:30 to 2:00 PM, and one from 4:30 to 5:00 PM. I have a shortcut on my iPhone that, at 3pm, automatically adds those time blocks for the following day.

In addition, Shortcuts can have more than one kind of trigger. With Zapier and Power Automate, the actions are triggered automatically by certain events or at certain times; they are not triggered by you manually. I have a screen on my iPhone that displays buttons for each of my Shortcuts. For those that are launched manually, all I must do is tap the button with my thumb. You can also trigger shortcuts to run at a particular time or when you arrive at a specified location (like your office or home).

In addition, my phone also pays attention to what I do throughout the day and often suggests shortcuts that can automate one of my repetitive tasks. More than one of my shortcuts has been created due to a suggestion from my phone. The key here is to look for automations and shortcuts on your phone or tablet that can run tasks on things that sync with your computer, like your calendar, e-mail, or task list. That way you can leverage an Apple automation app, even though you use a Windows computer.

Full On Apple Automation

Although most attorneys use Windows PCs in their practices, I cannot ignore those intrepid lawyers who use Apple products. This is especially because Apple has done such a wonderful job of implementing automation throughout all their systems. There are so many tools that I used to make my practice so much easier that I cannot fail to share them with the Apple users that pick up this book.

When it comes to the Apple ecosystem, there are several apps and utilities available, depending upon the types of workflows you're trying to automate. But in this section, I will talk about the ones I use every day: Keyboard Maestro, Hazel, and Automator.

Keyboard Maestro

You may have heard of the term macro in your computer use. A macro is nothing more than a series of computer instructions or keyboard commands strung together. The Keyboard Maestro app, published by Stairways Software, allows you to create, through a simple interface of drag and drop building blocks, a series of keyboard commands that can be executed all at once. This may not seem like much but let me give you an example.

In Microsoft Word on the Mac, printing an envelope for a letter takes several steps and keyboard clicks. You have to click on the Tools menu, select "Envelopes," and click OK if everything displays correctly. Then, when the window with the envelope is displayed, you have to click Command-P to print and then click on the Print button. That's 5 separate keystrokes (6 for me, because it keeps telling me to open the back cover of the printer). I reduced that to one by writing a Keyboard Maestro macro triggered by Option-P. I put an envelope in the printer, highlight the address in the letter, and press Option-P. Done!

Ask yourself how many routine tasks do you do in the course of a day that involve clicking around with your mouse or your keyboard in several steps that you could do blindfolded? Then do yourself a favor and, the next time you find yourself doing it, write it down on a notepad. I guarantee you that if you start on Monday, by the end of the week, you will have at least a dozen of them. Then imagine how much time you would save if one keystroke could replace all of those tasks that have several steps. It may only be a matter of seconds, but those seconds had up to minutes, hours, and days, over time.

Just go to keyboardmaestro.com. The company offers a free trial, but after that you can purchase it for only $36. That's next to nothing compared to the value of the time you will reclaim by creating automations with this program. If you are worried about the learning curve, an attorney in California named David Sparks writes video field guides for many different Mac programs, including this one. They cost about $49 apiece but they are invaluable as they do a great job teaching you how to use these programs. Just go to learn.macsparky.com to find out more.

Hazel

In a later section, I discuss how to transition to a paperless office. Part of having one is the regular scanning of incoming documents and correspondence. This can be very time consuming, not only in the time taken to scan the documents themselves, but in saving the PDF documents to the appropriate folder. This is where the program Hazel comes in. Hazel is an app that monitors certain folders and acts on new documents placed in them depending upon the rules that you set up. These act much like the email rules you may have set up in Outlook.

In the program, you identify the folder or folders you want Hazel to monitor. Then for each folder you set up rules to apply to each new document placed into the folder. Each rule acts as a set of criteria that the program applies to the document. Then it will take certain actions on any document that meets the criteria.

For example, let's say you're scanning a let
from opposing counsel in some litigation
You scan it, give it a name (e.g. "Smith
designate the monitoring folder you want
hit save. I use a folder on my desktop called
Hazel can then scan the contents of the do
set scanning for OCR, right?) for your clie
that name, it knows what matter folder to pu
use the word "letter" in the filename, Haze
in the correspondence sub folder. In this ex
done is scan the document, given it a name,
default folder. Hazel did the rest.

Hazel is a program published by a company
(www.noodlesoft.com). The program has a f
that it costs $42. Again, a drop in the buc
the value of the time you will reclaim by us
David Sparks also offers a field guide to teac
it, which costs $29.00.

Automator

Automator comes with the Mac operating
don't have to spend any extra money to get
to start using it. It also creates automation
integrated with the OS (not just apps), sc
customize your system. Have you ever pulle
for the app itself and seen an item called '
services can be provided by the program de
you can also use Automator to create your c

7. To find out what Services were added by apps, go to System Preferences, Keyboar
Then select Services from the list to the left.

is program is not quite for the faint of heart, and you ight want to hire someone to write the automations for you. vid Sparks does not offer a field guide for this program. the very least, I would get up to speed on the other tomation programs (like Keyboard Maestro) before you ckle Automator. Then start tooling around in it to see what can do. If you really want to get into the weeds, you can rt writing routines and Apple script, but that is a topic for other book.

e good news is that, starting with macOS Monterey, ortcuts is available on the Mac! So although Windows PC ers are limited to what Shortcuts can do on their mobile vices, Mac users can get that same functionality on their sktop or laptop computer. The great thing about Shortcuts that it is much easier to use than Automator, and it looks e Automator will be slowly phased out by Apple, so . . .

pp Recommendation

far, we have discussed automation features in other apps d apps that specifically create automated workflows. owever, there is an additional classification of apps that kes specific tasks and automates them, so that they take ew seconds, rather than a few minutes. As we have seen, ose minutes saved add up to hours over time and can make big difference in productivity.

ext Expander

xtExpander is a transformative app that has made a big fference in my law practice. Tedious, repetitive emails that

used to take me several minutes to draft and send, now take me seconds. Anytime I have text that is used repeatedly, whether it is in an email, a Word document, or a web page I am drafting, being able to turn a few keystrokes (called "snippets") into a few paragraphs, the task takes much less time. Thus if I were to type, for example, "oaddr" (the snippet), the program would expand that text into my office address without my having to type it.

Use Cases

I send routine emails all the time. When I do, I simply bring up my email program (either Outlook or Apple Mail), place the cursor in this subject field, and type a snippet. That snippet automatically expands to type in the subject, a table, and then the body of the email. If it is an email that needs to be copied (either too another person or my CRM-DSS) I typed the snippet into the CC field and expand it from there. The program automatically types in the email address of the person or DSS and then goes on to fill in the subject line and the body of the email.

But it doesn't stop there. I can put in various variables and customizations. For example, if I am sending a confirming email the business day before an appointment with a prospective client, the program will pause and ask me whether I want to refer to the appointment tomorrow or on Monday. In addition, the email talks about the subject of the consultation. TextExpander then pauses and offers me a pull-down menu to select the practice area. The customization and automation are incredibly powerful.

Letters and legal documents, as you know, often have standard paragraphs. By creating a TextExpander snippet, you can insert that language into the template (if you're creating a form) or the document itself if you're creating it from scratch. I find I am doing this very often in letters. How many times do we put into a letter a phrase like "sent via fax and regular mail?" I have a snippet for this, as well as "sent via email and regular mail," and "sent via certified and regular mail." Signature lines at the end of a letter can also be inserted.

Then there are web pages I'm writing. In my calls to action, I often identify my geographic service area. A call to action is key in all website content and must work to eliminate all those that you do not want to take that action. Therefore, I have a snippet that I type in, called "websac." This mnemonic refers to a web page snippet that sets forth the Service Area Counties.

TextExpander helps me way beyond the writing of emails, documents, and web pages. Website URLs can often be difficult to remember or take a long time to type. Snippets are perfect for this. My scheduling app, Microsoft bookings, has a long and involved URL for each separate bookings page comment, depending upon the type of appointment or meeting you are trying to schedule. Rather than try to remember it or type it in, I simply use a snippet.

Organizing & Remembering Snippets

The TextExpander program allows you to organize your snippets into folders in sections. However, once you have a few of them, and want to use them without looking them up in the TextExpander program, you need to create snippet names that will be easy to remember. The program helps with this by allowing you to create a prefix associated with each category in the program.

You then name the snippet you create, and the program automatically puts in the prefix. You saw this with the snippet for the service area counties in my calls to action. I used the prefix "web" for any snippet I use in website content. For emails, I use "EMT" for email template. For letters, I use "LTR," and for website URLs I use "//".

The prefix is then followed by an easy to remember name. So, for example, if I wanted to type in the URL for booking a 15-minute call, I use "//15mc". If I want to indicate that a letter is being sent by fax and regular mail, I use "ltrfax". Naturally you can create any mnemonic you want, whatever works. The point is to make it easy to remember.

One of the really cool things about TextExpander is that the software sends you an email once a month to tell you how many snippets you used and how much time you saved. This can be quite surprising, and I was amazed the first few times I received this email. Zapier does something similar to tell you how many zaps you used and how many tasks. However, the email does not translate that directly into time saved.

TextExpander is published by Smile Software, and you can get more information about it by going to www.textexpander.com. Unlike some other programs, you do not simply buy TextExpander. It is a subscription service that you pay for annually, but it is well worth it for the price. There are two main versions of the program, One for individuals and one for your firm. As of this writing, the former is priced at $40 per year, while the latter is $100 per year. Believe me, this small investment will pay huge dividends in your practice.

Need Help Automating?

Hopefully, all the tips and apps discussed in this section will get you fired up and started down the road to automating all of the repetitive and routine workflows in your practice. You will be so glad that you did it! Many of the tools I have discussed have an easy learning curve and are simple to implement.

David Sparks' field guides are awesome, no doubt. For little money, they will teach you all sorts of things about these programs that will get you started within hours. However, even with that, you may need assistance in using these tools to automate tasks within your practice. In addition, they don't cover all the tools I discuss here, like Automator or TextExpander.

If you need help learning to use these tools, finding ways to automate, and generally applying it to your practice, then check out the resources on my web site at www.StevenJRichardson.com or e-mail me at steve@stevenjrichardson.com to have a discussion on how I can help.

This book is all about systems. You will never accomplish what I did, or gain control over your practice, until you have systems for everything (and I do mean everything). There are many advantages to having these systems, which I will describe below, but in short, systems are what make the difference between the practice of law and the business of law. You must run your practice like a business if you are ever going to grow, have a sense of professional achievement, get control of your life, and have a better overall quality of life.

But before getting into the specifics of this, let me tell you the defining moment I had in my career that told me how powerful having systems can be.

How I Achieved a Clean Desk (For Myself and Everyone)

My first job as an attorney was with a collection firm in 1985. Work came to the firm from collection agencies over something called a "forwarders list." The matters would then go to in-house phone collectors who try and collect it. If that didn't get anywhere, they were referred to an associate attorney to file suit. The associates would handle the litigation, as well as all contact with the client/collection agency through written correspondence, whether the matter was in suit or not. Although the firm had recently implemented collection software, there were no computers on the attorneys' desks, and all of their work was still manual.

Secretaries would go through the mail, match it up with the corresponding physical file, and present rubber banded stacks of them to the attorneys to go through and dictate the next step triggered by that correspondence. I would get two or three stacks per day, and as you can imagine, the work piled up. I spent very little time actually practicing law, and a lot of time (and long hours) talking into a Dictaphone giving routine and mind-numbing instructions to staff on the next step. I would then take the cassette tape from the machine, rubber band it to that stack of files I had gone through and place it on a shelf for the secretary to type up the correspondence or the instructions. Lather, rinse, and repeat.

Systems are what make the difference between the practice of law and the business of law.

Every day was a constant struggle to stem the tide of those stacks of files and dictation. When any of the attorneys went on vacation, the deal was that they were not to leave before their office was completely clean and devoid of file stacks. Then, while they were on vacation, other attorneys in the office would pick up the slack and keep that office clean while that attorney was away.

One time after I came back from vacation, my secretary walked into my office and said, "Oh, by the way, while you were on vacation, I did your mail." She was a smart woman, and she figured out after a while what had to be done. When something is told to you, over and over, through a dictation machine, when A happens, do B, you learn the process. Life was much better after that.

Then at one point, a partner walked by my office and noticed how clean my desk was. When he asked about it, I explained what had happened. He got very excited and asked that I work with the rest of the secretaries, so that the other attorneys in the firm could do the same. I then sat down with my secretary and wrote up, for lack of a better term, a "user's manual" for the secretaries. It laid out a complete system, with all of the things that can happen on a file and all of the corresponding actions that had to be taken. In other words, a complete and exhaustive list of: When A happens, do B. With that manual came a binder of forms that were to be used for B (remember, this was the 1980s).

Things started running a lot more efficiently, and I was getting home much sooner. This incident cemented in my mind the importance of systems when it comes to the efficient and profitable practice of law (along with it being key to a better quality of life).

Why You Need Systems

For most of us, the practice of law consists of hustling to get the work in the door, and then grinding to get it out the door. We spend our days bouncing from one thing to the next, one file to the next, one urgent phone call to the next, and one court appearance to the next. We never take a step back to think more strategically about our business (and our practice is - and should be - a business), our goals, what we want to achieve, and where we want to be 10 years down the road. It's understandable why; we never think we have the time to do it. However, you must do it.

In his book, *The E-Myth: Why Most Small Businesses Don't Work and What to Do About It*, business coach Michael Gerber talks about Ray Kroc, the founder of McDonald's. Kroc realized that his product wasn't making hamburgers; it was the business that made the hamburgers, of selling the exact same one, whether that was in Philadelphia, Pennsylvania, or Omaha, Nebraska. He had the entire business, every step, mapped out and systematized. This made his business easy to grow and scale (and franchise), while maintaining the same quality. With the proper systems in place, everything else took care of itself, and he had a nice little money machine.

But you're not selling hamburgers; You're providing legal services. So what do these systems mean to you and why do you need them? The answer lies in the benefits it provides to any business that has them, as you will see.

SYSTEMS ALLOW YOU TO DELEGATE

Let's face it, attorneys are control freaks. I know this because **I'm** a control freak! We don't think anybody can do the job as well as we can, so we end up doing everything. We not only grind out the work for the client, but we also answer the phone, pay the bills, do the filing, do all the purchasing, and all the things that really do not require an attorney to get them done. As Michael Gerber says in his book, "If you don't have people, you don't have a business - you have a job." Thus, if we are ever going to gain control of our practices and have a profitable business that we enjoy running, we need to have people, and we need to delegate tasks to them.

Having systems in place makes it much easier for we, as control freaks, to delegate tasks to others. In those systems, if they are properly laid out, we provide step-by-step instructions on how to complete the task, and more importantly, how **we** would complete it. This not only makes you more comfortable that it will be done correctly by someone else, but also makes the staff person more comfortable because they know, as long as they follow the steps you have laid out, they will do the job correctly and not be criticized for doing it incorrectly.

> *If you don't have people, you don't have a business - you have a job.*

Systems Make it Easier to Manage Your Business

If your law firm does have staff, you know how complex managing them can be. There are all sorts of personalities, work ethics, and skill levels. Some employees are stellar, and you fear the day they decide to leave, while others are a constant source of stress and you fear the day you have to fire them. But having detailed systems in place makes it much easier to find good people, onboard them, and replace them should they leave or get fired.

Traditionally, when we look for employees, we look for people with experience. In a lot of ways, we want them to know how to do the job, so that they can be productive on day one and require very little, if any, on-boarding. However, with said experience often comes some bad habits and bad work attitudes ("this isn't how we did it at my old firm"). But with good systems in place, you can focus a lot less on experience, and more on whether they have the personalities and skills that would allow them to adopt and follow those systems that you put into place.

Having systems allows you to manage the process, not the people. People are too unpredictable; people are too variable in their personalities. People get sick, people go on vacation, and people have personality conflicts with other people. The only consistency you can count on is in your systems. Managing the systems instead of the people allows you to be sure that the good employees are doing the job the way you want them to and know whether the bad employees need to be replaced because they are not. Having easy systems to follow allows other people to take over when someone get sick, goes on vacation, or leaves the firm.

Systems Provide Quality and Consistency

Without systems in place, you will never know whether you have consistent quality of work from one case to the next. If you do things by the seat of your pants, or worse, your staff does, you cannot effectively control the quality of the work product. You need to determine the hallmarks of good quality legal work and a client-centric practice and then make sure there are systems in place for everything you do in your office to ensure that these hallmarks are met. This means having a system in place for everything that happens on a file, or in your office, from the time the initial intake is done with the potential client to the time when you complete the work, close the file, and hope that they will refer other clients to you.

We are human beings; we seldom do the same task exactly the same every time. Thus, without systems, it is impossible to maintain consistency. In addition, systems help to prevent mistakes. You are far less likely to forget a step in the process if all of them have been carefully laid out for you in advance. When you are doing consistently quality work, you build a reputation with your clients, as well as your colleagues in the legal community, and that good reputation will lead to referrals, more work, and growth. In short, systems help you to build, establish, and maintain your brand.

Systems Provide Efficiency and Profitability

Good systems involve automation, which I will address in more detail later in this book. When you automate repetitive tasks, you not only provide the consistency in the quality of the work product, but you're also able to do it in less time. Computers are a lot faster than you are, and they follow instructions much better (although they follow them explicitly, and to the letter, so you need to be careful to get it right when you do the automation). So even if you, or your staff, were following the system, in many instances it would take longer to do than if your computer did it for you.

Systems that involve and incorporate automation clearly make you more efficient, and therefore more profitable. You and the members of your staff are able to do more work in less time, which is always a good thing. I get into this in more detail in the automation section, but I wanted to mention it here, so that you can see it as part of the bigger picture.

Systems Let You Go on Vacation

In his book, *The Four-Hour Work Week*, Tim Ferris points out the importance of being able to remove yourself from your business. If your business is able to run without you, then you can generate revenue that isn't tied to your time. By having good systems in place, all of the work of your practice that can be delegated to a non-attorney (or an associate attorney in your office) can be governed by explicit guidelines that allow you to be sure that the work is being done properly without you being present.

Let me ask you this: When was the last time you took a vacation? When was the last time a vacation was more than a long weekend? If your practice is such that you feel that, if you ever left, it would fall apart, only having systems is going to change that. Managing your firm when you're not there is also easier because you are not managing people, you are managing the system. Delegating your work to people that can follow a well laid out system is the only true way of having a law practice and a life.

In addition, if you follow through on virtualization you will be able to work from anywhere. You can check in once per day from your laptop just to make sure everything is running smoothly. However, if you have good people, well-trained in your systems, they should know what to do 90 to 95% of the time, and not need your input.

Systems Create Equity

When it comes to the finances of your law firm, most attorneys concentrate on two numbers: revenue and profit. Is enough money coming in, and is that money covering expenses to the point where it is putting money into your pocket every month? But, there's a long-term financial number that very few attorneys think about: the equity in your firm.

Let me ask you another question: what is your exit strategy? Do you see yourself as ever retiring? Have you been able to put aside money towards retirement? Do you see any value in your practice that would allow you to sell it upon your retirement? Now the ethics rules in various states differ on the sale of a law practice, and many attorneys think that they can't sell it at all. They see the value of the firm as being the clientele. However, I suspect all jurisdictions hold the ethical position that the law firm does not own the file or the matter; the client does. The client has the ultimate decision on representation. Therefore, what are you actually selling when you sell your practice? The building (if you own it)? The furniture and fixtures? Your brand (if you have one - and it isn't tied to you)?

But if you are selling a practice that has a turnkey system for every aspect of the business, that will allow a new owner to step in while you step out (just like employees you have had over the years), that can have tremendous value. The attorney or attorneys coming in does not have to go through the laborious process of creating their own systems; you already have them in place for them. Therefore, systems provide great value and equity for your business should you decide to sell it.

SYSTEMS FOR YOUR PRACTICE

So, at this point, I hope you understand and appreciate the importance of systems in your law practice. Having them is the only way you can transform your law practice into a law business. Although you should have systems for every aspect of your practice, in this book I will lay out and discuss for you systems that address:

- Efficient management of time to allow you regain control of your practice
- Automation to free up time and allow you to be more efficient

who has traveled that path before you, then feel free to reach out to me through my website at www.StevenJRichardson.com for more resources and to schedule a call to discuss your needs and how I can help.

Chapter Three

Finding Your Ideal Client

Introduction

Before you set out to write one word of content for your web site, you need to have a very clear idea of who you are writing for. Who is your audience? Who is your perfect client? One of the biggest mistakes that salesmen make is that they try to sell to everyone. Every person they meet is a potential buyer. However, that is not the case at all.

I spent quite a bit of time in the previous section talking to you about your time and ways to ensure that you don't waste it (or have it stolen from you). If you try to sell to everyone, **I guarantee that you will waste a good bit of time.** Why? Because you will spend time talking to the tire kickers, the difficult people, the ones that are never going to hire you (or can't afford to hire you). The most efficient use of your time is to talk to the people who:

- Already know that they need your services
- See the value of it for the price you charge
- Can afford to pay for it
- Are already ready to hire you?

By having clarity on who your ideal client is and writing content to attract them, you will also repel the, shall we say, "less than ideal" client. This is the best, and most efficient, use of your time.

It's not just about your time, though, is it? How much stress and anxiety do you have in your life that is caused by bad clients?

You know, the unreasonable ones, the demanding ones, the ones that are never satisfied and are always complaining? How often have you heard the saying: The practice of law would be great, if it weren't for the clients? Imagine what your life, and your practice, would be like if you just represented your ideal client?

But what is your ideal client?

Getting clarity and focus on this is more involved than you think. I was coaching a personal injury attorney a while back, and I asked him: Who is your ideal client? He responded: Someone who's been in a car accident! I said, really? Are you sure? I asked him (and he answered):

- Do you want the driver who rear ended someone? (No, because he is the party who is liable for the accident)
- Do you want the driver who got into an accident, but only sustained some cuts and bruises? (No, because he doesn't have significant injuries, and his damages would be next to nothing, if any at all)
- Do you want the driver who was hit by someone who has lousy auto coverage, or no coverage at all? (No, because neither my client nor I will get paid or only be paid a fraction of the actual damages)

How often have you heard the saying: The practice of law would be great, if it weren't for the clients?

All of those people were in car accidents, but not all of them were his ideal client, and all it took was asking those three questions. He knew then that he had some thinking to do; he

) YOU GET CLARITY?

eveloped an exercise for the members of his Ops marketing mastermind group. It contains teps that need to be taken for each of your (and ideally any sub-practice areas as well). ps are:

ıd describe your perfect client

ne benefits, and the benefits of the benefits, of ce

y on what your service is and does

ll objections to retaining your service

addresses the characteristics of your avatar ver, as you can see, that is just the beginning hat you need to know in order to write killer must also:

n the benefits (and the benefits of the benefits) rvice

ctly how that service provides those benefits

ıll of the objections your potential customers ıg with any points of friction there may be, that ıem from retaining you

AMPLE

this is not enough. Having examples helps, so I low how I did the exercise on one of my services,

still needed to drill ‹
to his "avatar client,"
further would mean

- Is he/she marri
potential client's
- Are there childre
- Does he/she hav
large income rep
temporary or pe
- Was he/she a pas

The list of questions

The more you drill
that can drive your
check all of the boxes
produce leads that w
in a shorter period o
sifting through the ba

CRAFTI
CLIENT

So much for theory,
you need to have cla
gaining this clarity? N
information to write
that lead? Well, I'll tel

HOW D

Dave Frees
Business Blac
four critical
practice area
These four st

- Identify
- Identify
your serv
- Get clari
- Identify

The first pa
client. Howe
of knowing
content. You

- Be clear
of your s
- Know ex
- Identify
have, alc
prevent

FOR EX

But knowin
will review b

so you will have a clearer idea of how this works and how it can help you in your marketing.

I am primarily a bankruptcy attorney, although I also handle traffic and DUI cases, student loan issues, and collection defense/debt payment restructuring. When I sat down to do this exercise for my bankruptcy practice, I didn't just stop at "people who have loads of debt, few assets, and can't pay their bills." I dug a lot deeper because I wanted the "ideal" client for me. This is what I wrote.

MY AVATAR IS . . .

- highly organized men and women
- age 30 to 65+
- with good educations and technical savvy
- with computers and access to the Internet
- living in Burlington, Camden, Gloucester, Salem, or Cumberland Counties
- with general unsecured debt in excess of $15,000

What's important here is why I put down each of these factors.

Highly organized men and women. The last thing I need is a client that brings in a rat's nest file of bills and other documents that I (or my assistant) need to sift through. That's a waste of time and lowers profitability on a flat fee! I want them to bring in nicely organized, sorted, and labeled documents that will be easy to review.

Age 30 to 65+. A slightly older client will have had more time to run up debt that he/she can't pay back, have accumulated assets (like a house) that they need to protect, and have enough in income or bank balance to pay my flat fee (although that is not always assured).

With good educations and technical savvy. I run a highly efficient paperless practice in the cloud. I use a secure client portal for the client to input the necessary information for the bankruptcy petition. I deal in scanned (not paper) documents, as they are easily stored and accessed (especially by my assistant, who is in Kansas). I want the client to be comfortable using the web portal and have a scanner that can be used to scan and upload the necessary documents as PDFs. Their taking pictures of the documents with their phones is okay, but less than ideal.

With computers and access to the Internet. Although referrals are good, I like them to have done their research before coming to me. This makes them more comfortable with filing the bankruptcy and thus more ready to retain me. They don't still have to "think about it." They also are more likely to have read the content on my web site, and as such, I have built the authority necessary to them hiring **me** as opposed to someone else.

Living in Burlington, Camden, Gloucester, Salem, or Cumberland Counties. It's no good my talking to them to handle the bankruptcy if they don't live in my geographic area.

With general unsecured debt in excess of $15,000. It doesn't make sense to file bankruptcy and spend the money on the fees and costs of same if you only have a few thousand dollars in debt. I want the potential client to be struggling unsuccessfully with a mountain of debt, so that they will be more likely to see the benefit of filing bankruptcy.

So as you can see, a lot of factors come into play regarding your avatar client that can have nothing to do with "whether they have a good case." You need to give a lot of thought as to the characteristics of an ideal client. But that is only the first step of the exercise.

I Confer These Benefits (and Benefits of the Benefits)

Here you set out for the potential client what's in it for them. If you don't communicate clearly the advantages of retaining you, you make it far less likely that they will. You must set forth the benefits of your service, as well as the benefits of the benefits.

Now what do I mean by that? Well, the benefits of filing bankruptcy could be listed as:

- Ridding themselves of credit card debt, medical bills, and personal loan balances
- Wiping out motor vehicle surcharges in order to restore a driver's license
- Saving their home from foreclosure
- Paying back tax debt over time

These are the things that you, as the lawyer, see as the benefits of the service you provide. But you also need to get into the heads of your potential clients. They may understand on some level these benefits, but that is not truly what they are

Here is your opportunity to address these objections from the very beginning and inoculate yourself against them.[8] The more detailed the list the better!

I Can Help!

So, as you can see, there is a lot of work to be done before you even start writing the first piece of content for your web site. It isn't all about search engine optimization and getting on the first page of Google. It's about what happens after they click on your link in the search results and read your words. Will it answer their question? Will it help them? Will it resonate with them to the point that they say, "This lawyer really gets it, understands what I am going through and what my needs are." I need to reach out to him or her right away!

The sooner you start taking these four steps for every service you provide, the better. Go through it once and see what you get. If you need help taking this exercise to the next level and really drilling down to get total clarity on what you do and for whom in order to write killer content, then reach out to me at steve@stevenjrichardson.com. I provide personalized coaching services to walk you through this and optimize your content to convert your avatar client!

8. I will discuss how to do this in the next section.

Chapter Four

Writing Content

Writing Content for Your Avatar Client

Okay, I hear you ask, having clarity on my perfect client, what I can do for them, how, and despite their objections, is all very well and good. But how do I use that information to improve my website content and marketing copy? I'm so glad you asked!

The information from the clarity exercise will enhance your copy and make it much more likely to convert if you weave it into the page in these key areas:

- Headlines
- E-Mail Subject Lines
- Body Copy
- Calls to Action

If you have this information in your head as you write, it will resonate. Again, some examples of this will help, so here are some from my bankruptcy copy.

Headlines and E-Mail Subject Lines

People have short attention spans and you need to grab that attention in a short period of time. That's why headlines and e-mail subject lines are so critical. You need to grab their attention, and then keep it, with your copy. So, based on the information from the exercise, here are a few of them:

- How College Graduates Over 30 Can Get Rid of $15,000+ in Debt
- Nearing Retirement But Can't Shake $15,000+ in Debt?
- What Internet Research Won't Tell Older People About Freeing Themselves from 5-figure Debt!
- You've Tried for Years to Pay Back Your 5-Figure Debt Load, But the Balances Never Seem to Go Down! It's Time for a Better Solution!

Notice how I worked in the age demographic in the first one. Those under 30 won't see the advantage of reading the content and moved on. You've repelled the ant-avatar. The same is true for those not nearing retirement or "younger people." Those that **are** of that age will see it as something more pertaining to them.

Use the headlines and subject lines to inoculate against objections from the very start! Here are a few of them:

- Does Your FICO Score Begin with a 5? Then There's Nowhere But Up After Bankruptcy!
- Find out Why Over 95% of Homeowners in NJ Don't Lose Their Homes When They File Bankruptcy!
- Most People Can't Repay Their Defaulted Credit Card Debt, So Why Are You Still Trying?
- Why Getting Rid of $15-$100,000 in Debt is Worth the Price and Far Less Expensive Than You Might Think!

1 and educating themselves. Check out this · bankruptcy:

can easily get overwhelmed by credit card debt, l bills, and other financial obligations. A sudden reduction of income can wreak havoc on your s, even cause you to fall behind on mortgage or ments.

sounds like you, you are probably dealing with a eal of stress brought on by worry, thinking you ver get out from under it. This can wear you down ly, and even be bad for your health.

ou wish there was a solution?

ankruptcy can lift that weight from your shoulders, ou to imagine a future in which you needn't fear ank account being levied or your wages garnished.

ne a future where, instead of trying to scrape er a credit card payment, you can leave for a y weekend at the beach, go out to dinner at a nice ant (one without trays or disposable drink cups), something nice for your kids!"

aragraph speaks to their situation and offers an t shows them it isn't their fault. The next paragraph dges the effect it is having on them and that they g for a solution that works for them. The rest of the n't talk about the benefits of filing bankruptcy, but eper to the benefits of the benefits, using the word They then can't read the copy that follows without it happening to them. This is very powerful!

People that have worrie
that I have identified will
subject lines. They will w
from me. You want to be c
the reader:

If you have a FICO score ir
much more than it already

There is a slim chance that

You aren't alone; most peo
so it's okay to stop trying a

So start thinking about h
objections to retaining you
in your web site content!

BODY COPY

The initial purpose of you
inform the site visitor, alo
an expert on the subject.
visitor may well say, "Thanl
answered my question. Bye!
you don't want and waste
speak specifically to those
you don't want.

In addition, your body cop
talk about the benefits, as w
of the service that you prc
and thinking about hiring

informatio
example fc

"Peopl
medic
loss o
financ
tax pa

If this
great
will n
menta

Don't

Filing
allow
your

Imagi
togetl
getaw
restau
or bu

The first
excuse th
acknowle
are looki
copy doe
probes d
"imagine
imaginin

Calls to Action

Write this on a Post-It Note and put it on your monitor: "Every page on your web site must have a call to action!" You need to tell them what to do next, what you want them to do, after reading your web page. This is your final chance to inspire your avatar to take action, while discouraging your anti-avatar from doing so. How do I do this with my bankruptcy content? Like this:

> "So if you live in Burlington, Camden, Gloucester, Salem, or Cumberland County, can't pay your 5-figure debt load, know that you need to file bankruptcy to deal with it, and are ready to take action . . ."
>
> "So if you want a fresh start in life, one with vacations and date nights, not credit card payments, worry, and stress, you want it now and are ready to take action to get it . . ."

In the first example, I lay out four criteria that must be met before they take the action I want. The site visitor must:

- Live in my service area
- Finally decided that they can't repay their debt
- Have already decided upon bankruptcy as a solution
- Are ready to hire an attorney to file one, not just talk about it

The second example takes a bit of a different approach. It inspires action by resonating the benefits of the benefits. The site visitor must:

- Want the benefits of the benefits of my service (honestly, who wouldn't?)
- Not just be thinking about it
- Want those benefits of the benefits now, not just some time the future
- Are ready to hire a lawyer

Notice how I left out what you want them to do. You would then fill in: Call, e-mail, fill out your web form, download your book, whatever.

Now that we have that out of the way, let's talk about what you should write about on your site.

Inspiration for Content

Coming up with ideas for content can be tough, but it doesn't have to be. If you are just starting out with your web site, then there is most likely a plethora of topics you can talk about. But after a while, after you have written about all of the obvious stuff, you can be left scratching your head, staring at a blank page on a legal pad, wondering what to write down.

Believe me, I feel your pain! I've gone through this myself, especially since my law firm web site now has over 600 separate pieces of content! I have asked myself, "What more is there to talk about?" But over the years, I have discovered these tricks to find ideas and topics and unlock my brain to new ways to create content. So that you don't have to go through this yourself, here they are.

The Brain Dump

As I said, when you are first starting out, it is much easier. You haven't really written about anything yet! So the best thing to do at this stage is to do a brain dump. Take pen to legal pad and write down all of the questions you get from clients in all of your practice areas. These are the ones you answer in just about every consultation, whether it is the initial intake one or in subsequent meetings with the client after you have taken the case.

After you have written down everything you can think of, put it aside and do it again tomorrow. Sometimes in those intervening 24 hours ideas occur to you. Try again and write down more. Once you come up dry again, if you have a secretary or paralegal, bring them into the process. Bouncing ideas off someone else in a brainstorming session often shakes loose other ideas.

What I love about this process is that what you are writing down are Frequently Asked Questions or FAQs. These, in my opinion, are the best kinds of content because your potential clients are most likely typing their questions, worded as questions, directly into Google. Thus all you have to do is play Jeopardy and phrase your answer in the form of a question. Ask the questions they are typing into the search window and then answer them!

The Uber Article

After you have worked through your initial list of FAQs from your Brain Dump, review them again and look for common themes. Many times they are interrelated and part of a bigger issue. Take a step back and see the bigger picture. That common thread can then become the subject of an Article in which you talk about the bigger picture.

This content should interest your site visitors because it brings to light things they may not have thought about when they asked their initial question. They too start seeing the bigger picture along with you. One way to do this is to come up with a "Top 5" list. It doesn't have to be 5 things, but odd numbers do work better (unless it's a Top 10, of course), so try a top 3, 5, or 7 list.

For example, for my DUI practice I wrote individual pieces of content for each of 5 separate defenses to a drunk driving charge. I then wrote a Top 5 Defenses article that had links to the more detailed content on each one! A potential client with a DUI charge may be searching on one issue that could raise a defense, but my article points out four others!

The Should Ask Question (SAQ)

This is a topic my buddy Dave Frees talks about quite a bit. Your potential clients have questions that occur to them as lay people. These are the issues as they understand them to be in relation to their case. But you, as the lawyer, know there are other questions they **should** be asking but aren't. Since they don't know to ask it, you need to raise it and answer it for them.

Time to go through that initial list again. Think about the question and your answer and think about whether there's another, less obvious to the layman but obvious question to you and put them on a separate list of SAQs. These can be used to leverage other content, as I will discuss in the next section.

But again, here's an example. I handle matters in New Jersey traffic court, which also handles minor criminal charges, what other states call "misdemeanors" (we call them Disorderly Persons and Petty Disorderly Persons offenses - don't ask). As a result, I have an FAQ on my site called "What are the penalties for a NJ shoplifting charge?" Certainly someone so charged would type that question into Google, and I stand ready with the answer.

But what if the potential client is a public employee? If they are convicted of shoplifting, they could lose their job! They probably don't know this, though, so they won't think to ask it, but they should. So I have an SAQ on "Can I lose my public job if I am convicted of shoplifting?" This makes the potential client more aware of the bigger problem (and more likely to hire the person who pointed it out). Put this question, with a link to the page, in a list of SAQs at the end of the content.

The Sales Letter

Most of the content on your web site is written to educate your potential client and convert them to paying clients. You are trying to teach them something and build your authority as an expert in the area. But, let's face it, you are also trying to sell them your services! Start thinking about your content and ways of talking about the same thing with a salesman's voice.

I'm not talking about a pushy sales pitch here; I'm talking about an approach to the subject matter. Consider what I discussed in the previous section regarding writing for your avatar or ideal client. Address each topic in terms of the problems or pain points it creates for the potential client, how what you do can solve the problems and remove the pain points and present the benefits (and the benefits of the benefits) of you're doing so. Look at the analytics for your content and see what the most popular pages are, then work to recast this first in this new light. Then move on to other content.

The CLE Seminar

This is one I recently started using. In New Jersey we have mandatory CLE, so I often sit in seminars learning new stuff and earning enough credits to keep my license. But I also invariably learn something that my potential clients should know, and thus get some content out of it for my website. So I go through my notes to mine for ideas.

So grab your CLE notes and review them. As you do, make a list of all the things that might make good content. Each one may be good for 300-400 words (not bad for an FAQ), but you may also get an Article out of it by tying it all together. After all, the seminar speaker did just that!

Once you have gone through your notes from previous CLEs, start thinking strategically about what future seminars you should attend. Look for ones that not only will keep you up to date on the law in your practice area, but also ones that are most likely to point out new content. Oftentimes the CLE provider will do a Top 3 (or 5,7, 10) Things seminar that would give you the FAQs a unifying article you need.

This happened to me not long ago. A provider in my area has a seminar on "15 DWI Defenses That Actually Work." Taking this class gave me 2 substantive credits and 16 pieces of content (15 FAQs and an Article). A home run!

Ask Google for Ideas

Huh? What? How can Google help you come up with ideas for content? Well, as I discuss in the next section, Google can help you word your question and suggest other topics. Have you ever noticed when you type something into the search window and the results come back, there is a section of the results page called "People Also Ask." Sometimes this is a rewording of your question (and you should pay attention to that), but sometimes it lists related topics.

As a test I conducted when I was writing this section, I typed the following into Google: "What are the penalties for driving without insurance." This is what I got back under the "People Also Ask" section:

- What happens if someone crashes into you without insurance?
- How long can you go without car insurance before being penalized?
- How long can I drive without insurance?

Write these down as they are worded on another list to use later when you are writing. They not only provide ideas for content, but more importantly, they tell you what people are already looking for!

Be Strategic in Your Writing

I have a confession to make. One of my biggest mistakes early on when I was writing content is not asking myself the right question about my topics. There are two key questions, but I was only asking myself the first one. Those questions are:

- What's in it for the potential client?
- What's in it for me?

Clearly, I was asking the first one. I was writing content and answering questions that my site visitors would find informative and interesting. My site traffic reflected that in the number of visitors per month. But a good portion of that content was not answering the second question. Why is that question important? Because if you don't answer it correctly, you will end up wasting a lot of time writing content **that will never get you a client!**

Let me give you an example. I have a traffic court practice, representing people who get traffic tickets in municipal court. On occasion, the client will be someone with a learner's permit or what New Jersey calls a Graduated (Probationary) Driver's Licenses. Once they turn 18, they can apply for a standard license. But until then, they have restrictions on their driving privileges, and if they violate them, different penalties apply, depending on the offense.

Well, I thought it would be a good idea to write some FAQs on what a learner's permit and GDL were and what their restrictions were. Hey, it's what people might be interested in, it's in my wheelhouse, and it's another piece of content I can add to my site in the never-ending effort to Feed the Beast.

The outcome? I got literally thousands of hits to those pages every month, but not one of them needed to hire a lawyer; they just needed the information! I even had people call me occasionally to consult with me on it and ask about them, even though they hadn't received a ticket!! I finally "turned off" those pages one my site by not making them indexed on my page or searchable by Google.

Because if you don't answer it correctly, you will end up wasting a lot of time writing content that will never get you a client!

You know what happened as a result? The overall number of visitors to my site plummeted, but my conversion rate[9] went up because it is calculated based on leads divided by traffic. With the same number of leads and fewer site visitors, I had a more accurate indication of how well my site was converting them.

So when you go over your list of content ideas, ask yourself: What's in it for me? Will this page talk about a topic or issue that will be on the mind of someone looking to hire a lawyer (or in your opinion **should** be looking to hire a lawyer)? Be skeptical of anything that is merely informative to the visitor; this doesn't help you get more clients and more money, so you can pay the bills!

STRUCTURING AND WRITING YOUR CONTENT

So we've talked about how to identify what you should write about and how we can use the information gleaned from the

9. Percentage of site visitors that execute call to action by downloading a book, calling me, or filling out a contact form.

dense text with long paragraphs. Break things up into small bites that can be digested easily. When the page comes up, the visitor will likely scroll up and down through it first (I know I do), and continuous, densely packed paragraphs will put them off.

This is where headers come in. They break up the content and allow the reader to get a general idea of what you are talking about in your content. Make judicious use of them, but don't go overboard. When you put them in, be sure to:

- Use the H2 header format for major headings, and if you have subheadings under them, use H3. This is what Google looks for, and expects to see, in structured content[10]
- Use one or two important keywords in your headers and subheads. Google is looking for those as well.

So, as you can see, headers have two major benefits for your content: They make it more pleasing to the reader (and thus more likely to be read), and they help with SEO in getting your content found and served up by Google.[11]

Pull Your Visitors Deeper Into Your Site

Ideally, the visitors will be so impressed with the page they landed on that they call you right away! But this doesn't always happen. They will more likely either look briefly at your content and hit the back button on your browser (called

10. Any web content editor worth its salt will have a pull-down formatting menu that should list header sizes. HTML refers to them as H1 (the title of your page), and then H2 and H3 for headers and sub-headers within the content. Explore these options in the editor when creating headers.

11. By the way, did you notice that I have been using headers throughout this book? Did it help read and consume the content? Good! Then you see what I mean!

"pogo-sticking") or read your content and decide either that it did or did not answer their question and hit the back button (called "bouncing"). These two together constitute what Google calls the Bounce Rate of a page, and the lower it is, the better. The difference between the two is determined by another metric, Time on Page. If they bounced but stayed on your page for 2 minutes reading it, Google will conclude that they most likely found what they were looking for and rank your page higher.

But you know what's even better? Them staying on the page for 2 minutes and then not bouncing because they clicked through to other content on your site! That's why all my content, at the bottom, has a section called Related Topics. That section contains a bulleted list of at least three other pieces of content related to that page. Under the header, I state, "If you liked this information and found it useful, then you might like or need these others:" If they click on one of those, it doesn't count as a Bounce, and you build more authority with the visitor because they stayed after getting the answer to their question.

You can also have a section below that under the header Should Ask Questions (SAQs). Put them in a bulleted list below this language: "If you're interested in this or worried about this or this was important to you, then you should be asking these other questions below that my smartest and savviest clients didn't know to ask:"

Have a Call to Action

Every single piece of content on your web site must have a Call to Action (CTA). This is your opportunity to tell your site's visitor what you want them to do next. You should have one or two, but really no more than that. If you give them too many options, they will balk. There is a well-known saying in marketing: The confused mind always says No. So make your CTA clear and concise.

You should use the CTA to narrow the funnel, to weed out the non-avatars and tire kickers. Yes you want them to call or e-mail you, or fill out an intake form, but only if they are the client you want. It should contain language from the clarity exercise to do that.

One thing I do to ensure that they are in my geographic area is to ask for their zip code. It is a small ask (I don't request their full address), and it gives me valuable information about where they are and if they are a qualified lead. Fortunately, in New Jersey, the state is divided into the "08s" and the "07s." Southern New Jersey (where I am) has zip codes beginning with "08," and North Jersey (not in my geographic area for most services) has zip codes beginning with "07." Thus looking at the first two digits of the zip code tells me quite a lot, then I can zoom in further with the third digit. This may well not be as simple in your state, but it will tell you where they are with a quick Google search.

But they may not be ready to hire you yet, or even talk to a lawyer. So give them an alternative. Have a second CTA that directs them to download some sort of lead magnet, like a book or a report. The key is to get their contact information, so that you can market to them (which I will discuss in the next section). They may not be ready to call or retain, but with a name and e-mail address, you have multiple future opportunities to get in front of them and convert.

Have Several Ways for Them to Reach Out

A site visitor can e-mail you, fill out an intake form for a lead magnet, or call you. Each lead will have a preferred way to communicate, so be sure to cover all the bases. One way that has been proven to work is Chat. Many third-party vendors, like the one I use, Ngage, will provide a chat option so that a site visitor can talk to a real person (beware the chat bot), who can capture important information according to a script you provide, and put that into your CRM. Now you can respond to them and put them into an e-mail campaign (discussed below).

Have a Way to Track Your Marketing

No matter what you do in your marketing, you need to be able to track how it does. Is it working? Are people responding to your call to action once they read it? If you don't know the answer to these questions, you could spend immeasurable time and money and have no idea of whether it works. Naturally, if they fill out a contact form or download an offer, you will know that the page they were on worked. But what if they call?

You should have a tracking telephone number unique to your particular marketing campaign. I have one that appears on every page of my web site. If someone should pick up the phone after reading one of my landing pages and use that number, the call gets logged into my CRM. My website provider, Foster Web Marketing, provides me with the number (and rules of your jurisdiction to make sure that what you do on your site is in compliance and, if necessary, word your Privacy Policy accordingly.

Be Strategic in Your Writing

Once you have a list of content topics and have determined that there is something in it for the prospect as well as you, you need to plan the writing and publication. You need a content calendar.

You are going to be dripping out this content over time, so you need to map it out. When you first start your site, you will publish a lot more per week as you establish yourself with Google. Then, you can slow down a bit and publish 3 to 4 times a month (essentially once per week). If you are consistent and do this properly, then Google will see you as a site that is regularly updated with content and, if it finds the content to be good (people are searching for it and either not bouncing away or staying a short period of time - pogo sticking), it will rank you higher in the search results (i.e., closer to, or on, page 1).

My content calendar maps out multiple types of content over time. I try to do one piece of written content per week and one video a week. I also have a podcast that releases a new episode on the second and fourth Friday of every month. The show notes for the episode add a page of content to the site (which helps), and each episode has an audiogram (a video with a 60-70 second audio snippet to tease the episode and spark interest). The point is, there are regular updates all the time.

What you use to create the content calendar is not important; having one is! You can use an Excel spreadsheet (like I used to) or an app like AirTable, Asana, or Microsoft Lists to keep track. As part of my Sunday morning routine, I look over the content calendar for the coming week, add tasks to my task manager to create it, and block time on my regular calendar to get it done. That forces me to address it on the day and makes it more likely, when things get busy, that the marketing will get done.

Your content calendar should also include social media posts on your various platforms. List what you are going to post, with one entry for each platform (be it Facebook, Twitter, LinkedIn or Instagram). You need to be strategic with that aspect of your marketing as well. Don't leave it out or fail to plan for it!

I Can Help!

Producing content that gets found and converts, on a regular basis, is not easy. As you can see from the discussion in this section, there are several important steps that you need to take, consistently, to do this successfully. The good news is you are not on your own! I provide consulting services to assist attorneys in:

- Crafting content that speaks directly to your avatar client
- Writing targeted content that converts
- Tracking and testing marketing copy to do more of what works and less of that doesn't
- Laying out a strategic content campaign to build the authority of your site

Lead Magnets

All of your website content and marketing must ultimately ask the reader to do something; there must be a call to action. Without one, your content really serves no purpose and does not help you get new clients. The mistake that most people make in their marketing is assuming that the call to action must be for the person to call you. That is not always the case, and often the reader is not ready to talk to a lawyer; he or she is just in the information gathering stage. Although you ultimately want them to call you, make an appointment, and retain you, you must not jump to this as your go-to call to action.

But then what should your call to action be? The goal should be for you to convince the reader that they need to raise their hand, whether it be by calling or by downloading something. The download is called your lead magnet. It can take many forms and need not be that complicated or long. It just has to be something that your site visitor wants enough to give you their contact information in return for it. For me, lead magnets come in three basic forms, and I will go through each one of them below.

Simple Checklist or Top 5 One-Sheet

The first is a simple one sheet that contains something like a checklist or a top five, 7, or 9 list of important points. This could be something easy to put together and create a PDF. For example, if you handle residential real estate transactions, you could provide a list of all the things a buyer/seller should do in order for the closing to go smoothly. You could have one for the buyers and one for the sellers. Anyone buying or selling at home should see the value in this.

A colleague of mine, Joe Pardo, is a profit growth specialist and consultant for businesses. His lead magnet is a free guide called his sales rocket. It consists of five proven methods to increase your sales. You can get it in return for your name and email address. This is an excellent lead magnet for two reasons. First, it provides the site visitor with information they want to have and will be interested in reading it. Second, as a profit growth specialist, this lead magnet allows Joe to demonstrate his expertise and authority on the subject, giving the lead a taste of the kind of advice they can expect to get if they hire him.

REPORT

Then there is the report. This is a short document, maybe 5 to 10 pages, that provides your site visitor with a lot more information than they would get in one of your website articles or FAQs. This is your opportunity to take a much deeper to dive on a subject that you discuss in a more piecemeal manner on your website. It also allows you to provide more information to the visitor without going to the additional work of writing a book. Naturally, while a book would be a more detailed discussion of a topic (and may cover an entire practice area for you), the report is a lot less work.

For example, part of my practice involves doing expungements of criminal records. I have various articles and FAQ's on my site that deal with expungement topics, including:

without saying a word. Oftentimes, at the end of the interview, I will put pick up that copy of the book and hand it to them to take home.

I do this mainly in instances where the client has not decided to retain me yet and will be leaving without signing an agreement. This often happens with married couples where one spouse meets with me. I will then hand them the book, saying, "I'm sure your spouse will have a lot of questions when you get home. I trust that all the answers will be in this book." I have found this to be very powerful in converting leads that I have met with. I'm the bankruptcy attorney who wrote the book on it. You should consider doing the same.

Multimedia Lead Magnets

But your lead magnets need not be just the written word. They can be more multimedia. For example, you could create a series of videos on your YouTube channel that are marked private, and thus not available to the world on a Google search. If you are personal injury attorney, it could be a video course about how to make an insurance claim after an auto accident. Essentially, it could be a how to course on a lot of tasks that people struggle with when they have a legal problem. You put them together on YouTube in a playlist, and then provide the link URL to that list upon their filling out the contact form on your site.

How about audiobooks? You could create sound files of you reading from your book, and they can listen to it on their drive to work or at the gym. Audiobooks are becoming more and more popular and having one would help to distinguish you among the competition.

Chapter Five

Designing Better Campaigns

Introduction

Writing content that gets you found and gets you on the first page of Google is only the first step in your online marketing campaign. Many SEO companies fall short in their promises when they say that they'll get you on page one of Google, because they don't understand that that is not enough. You need to write content they will engage your site visitor, spark interest in your services, and get them to take action.

But even getting them to act isn't enough; you need to tell them what action to take! For this reason, every piece of content you write must have a call to action. You must tell the reader what you want them to do. This is because your site visitors are essentially invisible. They come, they read your content, and they go; you never know who they are. This will continue unless you give them a call to action that compels them to raise their hands. This gets them to identify themselves and get them onto your list of potential clients.

Once they are on your list, you can market to them further. These are people that were not only interested in your content, but they were also interested enough to act in some way and give you some information about themselves. Capitalizing on this information through an email marketing campaign is critical to your success. You have now been given a further opportunity to sell them. You sold them on your content; now it's time to sell them on your services.

but should rather aim to inform an engage. If you push too hard, you will get pushed back.

Be a Steve, Not a Stu

The best guiding principle I can give you for your overall marketing comes from an independent film that was released in 2000 called *The Tao of Steve*. This was a movie about a man who, while in college, discovered a foolproof way for picking up women. He called it the Tao of Steve because he saw the name Steve as being representative of the quintessential man (Steve Austin, Steve McGarrett, Steve McQueen).

Let me be clear; I am not advocating for this system's use as it was originally intended, nor am I expressing any approval of that. In fact, the main character in the movie realizes at the end that the Tao of Steve is not about picking up women at all, but about being a better person. One must also recognize and accept that sales and marketing are all about creating attraction and commitment, and thus its guiding rules can be applied very effectively in that context.

The Tao consisted of three basic rules that must be followed in a particular order, and if you fail to do so you were not a Steve, says the movie's main character, but a Stu.[12]

The first rule was to release your passions. In his context, this meant not going onto the date with the mindset of trying to sleep with a woman. You must release that passion and be yourself. In the business context, this means releasing your passion to sell. You're going on a date with the potential client and want them to retain you, but this cannot be part of your

12. The "anti-Steve" in many ways. The comparatives here are Barney Fife, Gomer Pyle, and Jughead Jones.

mindset in your marketing. I've read many times that people react negatively to a hard and pushy sale, thinking that the salesperson or business owner is desperate for the business. You do not want that.

The second rule of being Steve is to do something excellent in her presence (in that context to justify your worthiness). You must entertain her and impress her, so that she will become attracted to you. In the business context, this means building a rapport, as well as establishing yourself as an authority, impressing the potential client with your knowledge and expertise. Your FAQs and articles must give them the information that they need and speak directly to their emotions, fears, and concerns. In this way you build trust and authority (attraction) with the potential client.

The third rule of being Steve is to retreat. In the movie, this was done, in essence, to play hard to get, to confuse the woman and get her to pursue you. This rule is based on a simple philosophical observation that we pursue that which retreats from us. In the business context this relates back to the first rule, in that it has the initial appearance that you are failing to close. It gives the impression that you are so good at what you do that you are not desperate for money, do not need their business, and are not going to push. This is also where you work to repel your anti avatar and pique the interest of your avatar. You can put sentences like the following into your marketing:

- We do not work with everybody
- We are not for everybody
- We do not take on everyone as a client
- We are looking for clients that will be a good fit

Language like this can also be key in the call to action at the end of your content. If you will recall from the previous section on writing content for your avatar, I gave an example of:

> "So if you live in Burlington, Camden, Gloucester, Salem, or Cumberland County, can't pay your 5-figure debt load, know that you need to file bankruptcy to deal with it, and are ready to take action . . ."

This content "retreats" in the sense that I don't want to talk to you unless you live in my service area, have debt worth filing bankruptcy for, have already decided on bankruptcy as your solution, and are ready to file. In another sense I am telling them, don't call unless you really want me. This compels them to pursue someone who is retreating from them.

You should always be a Taoist in your marketing. Keeping that mindset will ensure far better success in expanding your business. As one of the characters in the movie says, as he transitions from being a Stu to a Steve, it's just three simple rules:

- Be passionless
- Be excellent
- Be gone

Do that in all things marketing, and there will be no stopping you!

Laying Out a Campaign

Mapping Out Your Drip Campaigns

Now that we have our mindset in place, we can move on to mapping out your email drip campaigns.[13] There are different kinds, and therefore different approaches you need to take in writing them. They are the relationship campaign, the offer download campaign, the contact campaign (a call or an email), the consultation follow-up campaign, the post retention campaign, and the file closing campaign. I will describe each of them below.

The key metrics with these campaigns are the Open Rate, the Click-Thru rate (you are providing links to content on your site), and the Opt-Out Rate (how many unsubscribe). A good open rate is considered to be 15-20% (although you should strive to get it higher), so measure your results accordingly.

Relationship Campaign

Building a relationship with the people on your list is critical. Therefore, I recommend that you have a general drip campaign for every lead, no matter what service they contacted you for, that regularly sends them an engaging email. Continue to build it by adding more emails on the end. I currently have a nurturing campaign that sends an email every 10 days for six months.

13. A series of e-mails planned out over time that are sent automatically to a lead on your list upon a triggering event (e.g., getting on to your list, downloading a lead magnet, filling out a contact form).

that I will get back to them within 24 hours, and provides them in the meantime with links to content on my web site (specific to the type of matter they are calling on) that they can read to answer some of their questions while awaiting my call. This satisfies their need for immediate gratification through a response while building my authority with them. In a very real way, I did get back to them immediately, even if they are waiting for my call.

These emails are extremely effective. The higher the percentage of recipients that receive the e-mail open it (and even better click through to my site using the embedded links) the better. Bearing in mind that a good open rate is considered to be 15-20%, here are the current open and clickthrough rates for each of my practice areas:

• Bankruptcy	66%	65%
• Collection Defense	69%	67%
• Drunk Driving	57%	92%
• Student Loans	76%	42%
• Traffic Court	68%	40%

As you can see, my leads eagerly receive and open these initial contact emails and click through to read a lot of the content I am providing to them. This helps to establish my reputation and authority with them even before the first phone call or consultation. You should definitely consider using these in your practice.

Consultation Follow-Up Campaign

Sometimes a client will meet with you but not be ready to retain. They need to "think about it." This often happens in my bankruptcy practice, as this is a step most people don't want to take and, despite my best efforts to repel anyone who is not already decided to file, they still end up failing to pull the trigger after the meeting. They may also be shopping around and talking to other attorneys, so I want to keep myself top of mind. It is therefore very important that you continue to follow up with this potential client after the meeting, so that they don't forget about you. You don't want that ideal client ultimately to end up retaining someone else.

To address this, I have a four-step e-mail campaign that is carried out over a 14-day period. The day after the interview, an email goes out thanking them for meeting with me and directing them back to my bankruptcy practice page for more information. Three days after that I send an email with links to download my three bankruptcy books to answer the questions they may have forgotten to ask during the consultation.

Since they may be shopping around, four days after that I send an email with lots of links to resources on my site about why they need a lawyer for their bankruptcy, how to find the right attorney, and what questions to ask an attorney in order to pick the right one. Naturally, I provide links to great answers to these questions to convince them that I'm still the right choice.

Two weeks after the consultation I send an email with links to lots of articles on my website talking about all the bad things that can happen by not filing bankruptcy or waiting too long to do so. This creates a sense of urgency and, hopefully, lights a fire under the prospective client and gets them to retain me. This campaign currently has a 49% open rate and a 12% clickthrough rate.

Sometimes the prospective client does not retain me at the initial consultation but does schedule a meeting for a future date to come back with money and the retainer agreement. Even though it appears that they are going to hire me, I do have a separate follow up campaign for that. It goes out over an 8-day period. The day after the interview, I send out an email thanking them for meeting with me. Four days after that, I send them an email with links to my other books to answer any further questions they may have forgotten to ask. This continues to inform the client and help reinforce the fact that they made the right decision.

Four days after that, and 8 days after the initial meeting, I send them the email with information about all the things that can go wrong if they wait too long to file or decide not to. The follow up meeting is usually within a week, and if that date passes without the client appearing, this still goes out, as it is designed to get them to reschedule. This campaign has a 68% open rate and an 18% clickthrough rate.

Post-Retention Campaign

The drip campaign should not end once the client actually retains you. These automated campaigns are also a great way to inform and update the client on the status and progress of their case, as well as manage expectations. I send out an initial new client welcome email that is generic. It welcomes them aboard and reminds them of my podcast on personal finance. This is then followed up a few days later with an email containing a survey to gather more information to feed into my ever-evolving avatar client profile. That campaign has an overall open rate of 61%.

That is then followed up by a campaign more specific to the service I am providing. For example, my bankruptcy campaign first sends an email explaining to them about my client portal that they will be using to provide information for the bankruptcy petition. It also provides a link to an article and information on how to use it. The second email provides instructions on how they are to submit documents to me. By their having clear instructions on how I need this to be done, it saves a lot of time once I receive them, as they are submitted in a way that facilitates my workflow in processing those documents.

The third email provides information on how to cut spending, so that they can better live within their means. This email provides links not only to articles on my website, but podcast episodes that discuss those topics as well. This provides a value-added service that goes beyond the preparation and filing of the bankruptcy petition. I am helping them to prepare for life after bankruptcy. The overall open rate for this campaign is currently 64%.

My drip campaigns for my traffic, drunk driving, and collection defense practices basically explain what I will be doing now that they've hired me, what happens next, and when they can expect to hear from me. This acts to reassure them that I'm getting to work right away on their matter and sets their expectations, so that they are not constantly calling and emailing me wanting to know what's going on.

Closed File Campaign

Don't forget about the client once you close the file! The completion of your handling of their matter does not mean the end of your relationship with them. Remember, you want them to retain you again and/or refer people to you. Therefore, you want to continue to nurture your relationship. There may also be useful information that you can share with them to help them move on after you have concluded their case. This is the kind of value-added service that should reap benefits in the form of repeat clients and referrals down the road.

For example, in my bankruptcy practice, I have a campaign that runs for 90 days after the file is closed. That campaign is as follows (with timing from the date the file was closed):

- Tips on rebuilding your credit. 7 days later
- Tips on cutting spending to stay within your budget. 21 days later
- A letter to upsell them for a will. 35 days later
- Tips on buying a home after bankruptcy. 60 days later
- Send them a copy of my bankruptcy book to give to a referral. 75 days later
- A reminder to check their credit reports to make sure that all their debts show as having been discharged. 90 days later

As you can see, I continue to nurture them along in life post-bankruptcy. Whereas other bankruptcy attorneys may think the job is over, and leave the client to their own devices, I continue to follow up and provide them with help. This is all done without me spending any of my time at all; it is all fully automated. This particular campaign is also very popular. It currently has a 53% open rate and a 33% clickthrough rate. Clearly, they're interested and what I have to say to them and the information I am providing to them.

me, there is no use keeping that lead on the list if it will not result a client or a referral. If they reached out for student loans or collection defense, I check the lead in 60 days to see what their open rate is on the email campaign. In other words, are they paying attention to me? If they are not opening anything and not listening to me, I delete them from the list.

Bi-Monthly Review

Beyond my daily review of the list of leads that came in the previous 24 hours, I do a more detailed review every 60 days. I looked to see whether they are engaging with me. Are they opening my emails? Are they clicking through to my content? In other words, have they shown an ongoing interest beyond their initial visit to my site?

Non-Leads. If I have classified them as a non-lead in a geographically dependent practice area, I delete them. If they are in a non-geographically dependent one and they are not paying any attention, I delete them. If they are in the latter group but paying attention, I mark them for review after another 60 days and monitor their engagement.

Warm Leads. If they are Warm Leads, I check to see whether they are paying attention. Have they opened at least 2 of the last 10 emails they were sent? If they did not, I delete them. If they did, I keep them or review in another 60 days. If they opened more than 3 of the last 10 emails, I sent them (i.e. At least a 40% open rate), I changed their tag from Warm Lead to Raving Fan. This allows me to segment my list and isolate those that are really paying attention to me.

Hot Leads. Then there are Hot Leads, both with and without addresses. If they're not paying attention, I tagged them Last Chance, which puts them in a special email campaign to try and warm them up. If that fails, I delete them in 60 days. If it succeeds, I keep them on. If they are opening more than three of the last 10 emails, I sent them, I tagged them VIP. This triggers an email campaign to them telling them they have joined my VIP Club, which entitles them to some additional benefits and content. The VIP list is much like the Raving Fan list, but this is a list of people most likely to retain me or refer business to me.

Client. If a lead becomes a client, they are tagged as a Client, and also receive a tag specific to the service I am providing. Is this a new client for a bankruptcy, a traffic ticket, a DUI, or debt collection matter? Each of these sends out a separate nurturing campaign telling them what the next steps are going to be in my handling of their matter. This helps to set expectations and keep them informed about the progress of their matter. Once leads become clients, they are never deleted from my list.

Unsubscribe. Also, as part of this review, I delete any lead that has unsubscribed from the list. They obviously do not want to hear from me further. However, if I have a Hot Lead with an address, I tag them Back Burner in order to segment a list of Hot Leads that could be part of a snail mail campaign at some point.

Leveraging Targeted Blasts

Now that your list has been curated and tagged, it can be weaponized. There is a great deal you can do with this list by properly analyzing the data and targeting your marketing message. I used the DSS tool designed by Foster Web Marketing for my website, but any CRM program you use (whether it be InfusionSoft, MailChimp, or something else) needs to have the capability of assigning multiple tags to a lead, along with strong search and filtering capabilities to manipulate the data in your list.

Let's say you're testing a new offer. You can draft a targeted email and then delineate your audience by having it sent only to members of your VIP list that reached out to you in that particular practice area. Those on your VIP list have a high open rate and are most likely to pay attention to the e-mail. If you get a response from them, you can try sending it to everyone else on your list for that practice area. It's all about getting the right content in front of the right leads on your list. You only want to send that marketing message to those who are most likely to respond.

For example, I have many people that reach out to me about bankruptcy or they download one of my bankruptcy offers, but not all of them are in the geographic area that I serve for that practice area. If I send out bankruptcy marketing material, I'm only going to want to send it to those tagged for bankruptcy that are in my service area.

On the other hand, the pandemic has made people more comfortable with virtual platforms like Zoom. In fact, studies are showing that potential clients don't expect to have to come to your office for meetings or to retain you. So now I am rethinking how I classify leads geographically for my collection defense and student loan practices. I no longer assume that those leads will not convert because they are too far away from my office. They might be willing to meet virtually (by Zoom or some other platform).

By having properly tagged leads, I can send a message to all those leads that contacted me for collection or student loans that live outside my geographic service area to talk to them about virtual representation options, just in case that hadn't occurred to them. This prevents them from automatically assuming that they are too far from my office to hire me, and as a result, not converting them from a lead to a client.

Having a Newsletter

In addition to campaigns and periodic blasts to your list, it is also a good idea to have a newsletter. I would recommend starting out having it as electronic, and then once you have built and curated a list of contacts, have a printed newsletter sent out quarterly. But let's talk about an eNewsletter here.

The most important thing about your newsletter is that most of it should have nothing to do with the law. Remember, you are building a relationship with the prospects on your list, so your newsletter should not push to sell. You can have content that talks about what you do, but it should not be any more than 1/3 of the overall content of the newsletter. Your CRM should have the capability to create email templates. I would use that feature to create a consistent look and feel and layout to the newsletter.

Everyone who reaches out to me that is a Hot or Warm Lead, no matter what the reason or practice area, gets my newsletter. I send it out twice a month on the 1st and 3rd

m doing
ince the

Freedom
ng fit for
. People
nt ways.
e people
senses.
hing," I
ok page,
eating a

wsletter
r story,
r forget
ason to
ring or

all of
key to
ime to
? Plus,
w you

haven't
ecided

kly is a little too much (and more
nthly isn't quite enough. It has a
y a message personalized to the

bout your newsletter is that most of
with the law.

rney and entrepreneur Ben Glass,
l their story." I often talk about
(to the extent that it's interesting
vhat's going on in the world (while
of politics), and generally try to
with the reader. Many times, I have
may say something at the end like
e. Hit the reply button and let me
usually get several responses, and
lerstand that these are not one-way
nversation.

content sections that I filled with
such as recipes, entertainment ideas
out daysoftheyear.com. You will be
ngs each day of the year is dedicated
what's being celebrated on the day
l and provide humorous information
vith clickable links through the pages

lat talks about what's going on in my
h I would recommend you have. My
ww.RichardsonLawOffices.com, but I
ain to point to the YouTube channel
LawOffices.TV. This makes it easy to

remember. This section allows me to talk up what I on the channel and promote the videos I've released previous e-newsletter issue.

After that, I talk about my podcast, the *Financial Podcast*. A podcast is not necessarily a good marketi every practice, but I have found that it works for m learn in different ways and consume content in differ Some people read, some people watch video, and son learn by listening. If you can, you should cover all th Finally, to follow the advice of "always leave them lau end with a lawyer joke. This then links to my Facebo and encourages them to engage with me there, cr community.

The most important thing is that you make the ne your own. Use it to express your personality, tell yo and provide the reader with useful information. Nev that it's all about them. You need to give them a re open and read your newsletter every time. If it's be uninteresting, they will unsubscribe very quickly.

Need Help?

Designing and implementing effective campaigns o these different types (including your newsletter) is marketing your practice successfully. But who has the design and lay out a campaign, and write all the e-mai the way you write the e-mails is just as important as h write the landing pages on your web site.

If your campaigns have been neglected because you had the time to create and maintain them, you have that you don't have the time or the expertise to do it yourself, or you just need help in getting it done, no problem! Just reach out to me through www.StevenJRichardson.com to schedule a no-obligation call, and take your first step towards better, more effective, marketing!

Chapter Six

Social Media

INTRODUCTION

Oh, great! On top of everything else you have to do (writing content for your website, shooting videos, and planning sophisticated and effective email drip campaigns), you are being told that you have to be on social media. So many marketing consultants and coaches count this as the "be all" and "end all" to marketing. I disagree, as would many other marketing experts. Social media is but one tool in your toolbox. You should make sure that you are using the right tool for the right job and that you are using it effectively.

BE STRATEGIC: WHERE IS YOUR AVATAR?

There are two main things you need to bear in mind when it comes to a social media strategy for your practice. First, you must be strategic in the social media platforms on which you participate. There are many of them out there, including Facebook, Twitter, Instagram, LinkedIn, Tik Tok, and SnapChat, with others being created all the time. But this is the question you must ask for each of these platforms: "Is this where my audience is?"

Go back to your avatar exercise and give some serious thought as to "who" in terms of social media. Where would these people be found? What age group(s) are you looking at? Boomers and Gen X'ers tend to gravitate to Facebook, while younger millennials and Gen Z'ers are on Instagram or Tick Tok. In my practice, I have a presence on Facebook, Twitter, and LinkedIn. As Instagram became bigger, I started looking into the platform and the demographics to see whether my avatar was there. My ideal clients tend to be older, and the research I did showed that the Instagram audience skewed to the younger population. For that reason, at least for the time being, I chose not to be on that platform (and quite frankly, three of them was enough).

As part of the ongoing research you do on your avatar, find out where they are on social media. Do you tend to represent businesses and employers? Then maybe LinkedIn and LinkedIn groups might be a better place for you. I cannot stress enough the importance of doing this first. If you don't, your efforts may be ignored, or worse, you will attract potential clients who are not your avatar, and you'll end up wasting a lot of time. Be where your avatar is.

Be Social!

The second main thing is to bear in mind that social media is social. It is a cocktail party, not a CLE seminar. Don't use it solely to blast out links to your content on a regular basis. Few, if any, will care. Worse, you will turn people off. When it comes to your postings, remember the first rule of being Steve: release your passions and don't try to sell them. Rather, be excellent in their presence by being helpful to them and contributing to the conversation. People hire lawyers they like, or refer other people to them, so this is your opportunity to get them to like you. Not only post your own stuff, but comment on other people's posts. Retweet or Like something. Get to know people. Get to know your audience. Get to know your pool of potential clients.

This is the part of social media marketing that so many people get wrong. Although I'm a big fan of delegating, and my assistant does handle a good part of my social media marketing, you really shouldn't hand off this task to someone else to handle exclusively. That person can handle your social media content calendar, which I will discuss in a later section, but you need to get out your phone on a regular basis, check your feed, and participate in the conversation. This is not something someone else can do for you. Follow these two rules, and have a consistent and strategic social media plan, and you will do well.

YouTube as Social Media

You've probably been told that you need video as a part of your marketing strategy. Oh great! Even more to do! But as I said earlier, people consume content in different ways, and having a video option can make all the difference. Many people, when they call me, will start the conversation by saying, "I just watched one of your videos." You cannot ignore this marketing opportunity. As YouTube can be considered social media, I'm including it in this section.

You should give some careful thought to your channel before you launch it in order to have the best chance of success. Don't just start filming yourself with your iPhone and hitting upload. Like everything else you do in your marketing, there has to be an overall strategy. So I am going to lay out in this section what you need to do.

Starting and Building Your Channel

According to Owen Hemsath (known as Owen Video) of the Video Marketing School, in building and maintaining your channel, there are four steps you need to follow in order to maximize your success, and each one is of equal importance. They are:

- Programming
- Production
- Promotion
- Progress

Let's look at these individually and see what you need to do in each of these steps.

Programming. This is your content strategy. Like building anything else, if you want to construct something that will last, you have to build it on a strong foundation. But laying out that foundation involves a good deal of thought and strategy before you first set up a camera. You need to come up with an overall concept and theme for that channel, then produce videos that will support it.

> *YouTube considers the minimum for success to be 1,000 subscribers and 4,000 hours of annual watch time.*

Believe it or not, according to Owen, search engine optimization is not the most important strategy for getting your videos found. Why? Because there are never enough people searching for your keywords to give you the momentum that you need to succeed in getting your videos watched. You should be talking about the things that the viewer **should** be looking for, and not necessarily what they **are** looking for. Another way of looking at it is, your videos are the SAQs, rather than the FAQs.

Google uses different algorithms for YouTube, says Owen, and good content will cause YouTube to put your video in with other similar ones to recommend to people. For this reason, you need to optimize your videos for views and watch time. Having a good number of subscribers is also important, but YouTube considers the minimum for success to be 1,000 subscribers and 4,000 hours of annual watch time. Once you have built up that momentum, good SEO will help make it better.

Production. This involves producing the best possible videos in the shortest amount of time. The process falls into three phases:

- Filming
- Editing, and
- Thumbnail design.

In the first two steps you should consider the structure of the video and make sure it is consistent every time. Consistency here will create familiarity with your viewer. There should be a similar look and feel to each episode. If you decide that changes need to be made to this, you shouldn't make them until after the first 10 videos are uploaded.

You need structure in your video as much as you need it in your written content on your website. Present the information in an organized fashion, so that your viewer may more easily follow along. Put headers on your videos at the beginning of each section and prominent print at the bottom. You can also use transition cards between segments. Just like your website content, your videos should also have a call to action. What do you want them to do when they finish watching? Have you noticed, a lot of successful web YouTube channels never fail to remind the viewer to Like the video and "click to subscribe?" You should do so too.

But as I said before, YouTube is social media. People can leave comments on your videos. This allows you to start a conversation with these people. I'm not saying you should give them legal advice or answer any legal questions, but this is a great way to build a community. Your video should, where appropriate, invite the viewer to post a comment; this gives you the opportunity to be social with your videos.

In addition to the description of the video on YouTube, you are given the opportunity to assign tags. Although SEO is not the be-all and the end-all to your videos, it does help, so you should pay attention to tagging. As with other social media platforms like Twitter and LinkedIn, tagging is important in YouTube. You want tags that have a high search percentage and low competition. When it comes to finding good tags and tweaking your videos, I must recommend the YouTube plugin TubeBuddy. You can get more information on it from their website at www.TubeBuddy.com.

I use TubeBuddy quite a bit in my videos to choose tags. One of the things it does is scan your description and recommend appropriate tags, which you can then select. If you type in your own tags, you can double click on them, and TubeBuddy will tell you how that tag ranks. There is a version of this plugin that is free, so I would urge you to check it out.

Believe it or not, the thumbnail[15] for your video is also critical. In fact, says Owen, you should create your thumbnail before you even shoot the video. The video content itself doesn't attract viewers; your thumbnail does. You should have a template that you augment for each video. It should also consist of four basic parts:

- Background
- A picture of you (preferably with the background removed, so you can lay it over the rest of the thumbnail image)
- Text
- An icon or graphic

If you're not clear on what I mean by this, just go to YouTube and look at all the thumbnails for the videos. Which ones spark your interest? Which ones really stand out among the others? Which ones would make you click, and which ones would you just scroll past?

Promotion. Once you have planned your channel and produced good content and eye-catching thumbnails, you need to promote that content. This should be done through a checklist, so there is some consistency in the way you promote each video after its release. Consider sending an email to your list telling them about the new video on your channel, including the thumbnail. Consider also whether you should do a targeted emailing or just send it to your entire list in bulk.

15. A picture or video freeze frame used to identify your video on YouTube and other video platforms. It is also the icon you click on to launch it.

Posting videos to your Facebook page and groups can have a decent effect early on. Ask your friends and family to watch the videos for a while and like them. You could also ask them to subscribe as well. However, remember that you want to have a lot of watch time to get your videos ranked; your friends and family watching it for a minute or so and liking it will not, ultimately, provide you with the momentum you need. Thus you should phase that out over time and rely on the YouTube algorithm to do the work. You should also share your videos in your networks as they exist today, as you have already built those up. Don't try to create a network from scratch just to promote your videos.

In the beginning, just keep making and uploading the videos; keep your head down and keep working. Consistent uploading of new videos to your channel is very important. Then, every time you meet new prospects, send them a note with a link to your video.

Progress. This means keeping an eye on your analytics. First off, look at your clickthrough rate. This shows how often the thumbnail appeared and what percentage of people that saw it clicked through it to watch the video. Then there is the watch time or average view duration. This shows a percentage, as well as a time in minutes, of how much of your video people are watching. With this information you have what you need to grow your channel. The more momentum you build, the more YouTube will recommend your videos to others.

Owen and his Video Marketing School have some great classes and coaching programs for being a success on YouTube. If you need help to become a YouTube star, check him out at www.thevideomarketingschool.com.

Content Ideas

So what are you talking about in your videos? Just like with your website, you have to come up with ideas for the content in your channel. However, this job is easier because you've already come up with the content ideas; you use them on your website! Go back over your list of FAQs and articles that you made on that yellow pad and think about how easily you could turn it into a video.

The website content itself can create the script for your video, as well as the topic. In addition, that text can also serve as the video description in YouTube, although for SEO reasons, you'll want to be careful the language is not identical in both places. Make sure to do some rewrites to make it more appropriate for the YouTube platform. How you write your copy is a little different for a standalone video that already provides the content for the site visitor. It can be more of a summary of the content or a list of time markers that can act as a table of contents.

Even better, while building your YouTube channel by putting up new videos, those videos can enhance your website content. Talk to your website designer about embedding your YouTube videos onto your landing pages that discuss the same topic. This gives your website viewers the choice to either consume your content by reading it or watching it. As such, those videos you're creating serve a purpose on two different platforms, not just one.

There is no guarantee that your videos will go viral, but strategic and consistent work to build and maintain your channel will get you the best chance of success.

Plotting out a Campaign

Just as it's important to have a content calendar for your website, it is also key to map out your social media strategy. While being social, you also need to bear in mind that the main goal of social media is to get the person to transition from your social media site and onto your website. But it is not enough to get them onto your site; You need to get them onto your list. Social media platforms come and go, and you have no control over them. But your site is yours, and once you get them there, there is more you can do to market to them.

Creating Community

One of the advantages of Facebook is the ability to create community, a place where the people on your list can get together and interact. Many law firms have a Facebook page to which they post content (either occasionally or on a regular basis). That does help to some extent. The problem is, this just creates another platform for your content, much like your website. You post there and hope that people will see it, like it, and comment on it. But with all the pages out there that Facebook users can like, it can be hard to get attention and maintain loyalty. You want to go beyond that and create community.

You need to do more than create a connection between you and the potential client; you need to create a connection among the people in that group. One way to do this is to create a Facebook Group and make it private. This keeps the group to the people who will get value from it and engage with you (along with other group members). The purpose of your group is threefold: to connect, to teach, and to learn. This is much easier to do with the community, because it is the connection that the member has with other members, rather than just with you, that will keep them coming back on a regular basis.

Having a Social Media Content Calendar

When it comes to what to post, coming up with ideas can be time-consuming. For that reason, many people get discouraged. However, a marketing coach I spoke with, Elizabeth Pampalone, teaches a great system for getting a year's worth of social media posts in one day. This may seem outrageous, but when you think about what she proposes, and the very nature of social media, it makes sense.

She recommends that you put out four to five posts per week on the social media platforms where your avatars are by rotating through four to five types of posts. Remember, not everyone in your audience is going to see your post on Facebook, Twitter, LinkedIn, or Instagram. Social media moves way too fast and is way too crowded for that to happen. Therefore, if you post the same thing more than once, few, if any, are going to notice that you're repeating yourself. As to the types of posts, they are as follows:

- **Fluff Posts.** These are links to interesting and informative resources on the Internet that relate in some way to your practice. As my practice consists primarily of bankruptcy, collection defense, and student loans, my fluff posts tend to be about personal finance. Get a list of 26 of them (preferably Evergreen content), then repeat.

CHAPTER SEVEN

FREEING YOURSELF FROM THE OFFICE

INTRODUCTION

If the COVID-19 pandemic has taught us anything, it's the importance of being able to work from anywhere. If your office shut down, then you had to find ways to make any location your office, not only for yourself but for your staff as well. Even if your office didn't shut down, being more virtual probably moved up considerably on your lists of priorities. That's why I wanted to talk to you in this section about my journey to virtual in the hopes that it will make the transition easier for you.

When I opened my solo firm in 2000, it was just me; I had no secretary or paralegal. I answered my own phone and my e-mails. I did everything for myself. So if I was ever going to be able to go on vacation or take a couple of days off, my office had to be wherever I was. My laptop went everywhere with me, and when smartphones started coming out, I got a BlackBerry (I have since moved on to an iPhone). I could check voicemail and return calls and respond to e-mails. I even set up a system whereby I could access my office computer remotely.

I truly believed I could work from anywhere.

If the COVID-19 pandemic has taught us anything, it's the importance of being able to work from anywhere.

But when the pandemic hit, I found out how wrong I'd been! If I was forced to work from home, there were several important things I still couldn't do. Not good! I could still access my office computer remotely, but it was a bit awkward and clunky,

Competence. This rule requires you to maintain the requisite knowledge and skill necessary for the task at hand. You must also keep reasonably up to date on the subject. Up until now, you have probably looked at this as applying to your various practice areas and keeping up on the changes in the law and generally knowing what you are doing. However, this is also being applied to all aspects of your practice that could impact the services you render for your clients.

What does this mean here? It means that you can't just hire a consultant to set everything up for you and "worry about the little IT details." Although you are not expected to be an expert on tech and IT in general, you are expected to verify certain aspects of the technology to be sure that it gets the job done properly. In short, you can't abdicate your responsibility to the IT guy; you have to know the basics.

Confidentiality. This rule basically requires you to make reasonable efforts to prevent inadvertent disclosure. The key word here is "reasonable." Did you do your due diligence with regard to vendor and platforms? When you chose your cloud provider, did you make sure that there was "end to end encryption" of the data? End to end means that once it leaves your computer through upload, it is encrypted in transit and encrypted on their servers. Make inquiries as to how good their on-site security is. Did the vendor just throw your files onto a hard drive in a third-party server farm, or is it their own facility with locked doors and limited access to the hardware? Be sure to ask good questions and get good answers.

Communication. Most jurisdictions, as far as I know, allow for the use of e-mail. People pretty much understand its nature and that it isn't very private. Besides, e-mail encryption is a pain! But if you are using cloud technology, be sure to

Introduction

If the COVID-19 pandemic has taught us anything, it's the importance of being able to work from anywhere. If your office shut down, then you had to find ways to make any location your office, not only for yourself but for your staff as well. Even if your office didn't shut down, being more virtual probably moved up considerably on your lists of priorities. That's why I wanted to talk to you in this section about my journey to virtual in the hopes that it will make the transition easier for you.

When I opened my solo firm in 2000, it was just me; I had no secretary or paralegal. I answered my own phone and my e-mails. I did everything for myself. So if I was ever going to be able to go on vacation or take a couple of days off, my office had to be wherever I was. My laptop went everywhere with me, and when smartphones started coming out, I got a BlackBerry (I have since moved on to an iPhone). I could check voicemail and return calls and respond to e-mails. I even set up a system whereby I could access my office computer remotely.

I truly believed I could work from anywhere.

If the COVID-19 pandemic has taught us anything, it's the importance of being able to work from anywhere.

But when the pandemic hit, I found out how wrong I'd been! If I was forced to work from home, there were several important things I still couldn't do. Not good! I could still access my office computer remotely, but it was a bit awkward and clunky,

own suite of productivity apps through the iWork platform. Dropbox, however, just stores your data. It has a lot of features that may be useful for you, so just don't write it off. But you will have to come up with your own system for using it with other apps, such as case management.

Office Platforms

The overall office platform you use for creating and editing documents must work hand in glove with your cloud storage. This decision may already have been made for you. If you already use Word and Excel extensively, then there's Microsoft 365. If you are an Apple shop, already familiar with the Pages, Numbers, and Keynote apps, then iWork would be better. The same is true of Google, if you have been using Workspace up until now.

The key element here is that you settle on a cloud solution that mirrors your practice in the virtual world. It must house all of your documents and make them accessible from anywhere, facilitate communication amongst the people in your firm, as well as your clients, and make sure all of it is secure and confidential.

If you are not already committed to one, then Google around for comparison articles and familiarize yourself with the pros and cons. I could do it here, but these services evolve and change, as features and interfaces change. Besides, what's right for you may well not be what's right for me, so . . . .

own suite of productivity apps through the iWork platform. Dropbox, however, just stores your data. It has a lot of features that may be useful for you, so just don't write it off. But you will have to come up with your own system for using it with other apps, such as case management.

Office Platforms

The overall office platform you use for creating and editing documents must work hand in glove with your cloud storage. This decision may already have been made for you. If you already use Word and Excel extensively, then there's Microsoft 365. If you are an Apple shop, already familiar with the Pages, Numbers, and Keynote apps, then iWork would be better. The same is true of Google, if you have been using Workspace up until now.

The key element here is that you settle on a cloud solution that mirrors your practice in the virtual world. It must house all of your documents and make them accessible from anywhere, facilitate communication amongst the people in your firm, as well as your clients, and make sure all of it is secure and confidential.

If you are not already committed to one, then Google around for comparison articles and familiarize yourself with the pros and cons. I could do it here, but these services evolve and change, as features and interfaces change. Besides, what's right for you may well not be what's right for me, so . . . .

Introduction

If the COVID-19 pandemic has taught us anything, it's the importance of being able to work from anywhere. If your office shut down, then you had to find ways to make any location your office, not only for yourself but for your staff as well. Even if your office didn't shut down, being more virtual probably moved up considerably on your lists of priorities. That's why I wanted to talk to you in this section about my journey to virtual in the hopes that it will make the transition easier for you.

When I opened my solo firm in 2000, it was just me; I had no secretary or paralegal. I answered my own phone and my e-mails. I did everything for myself. So if I was ever going to be able to go on vacation or take a couple of days off, my office had to be wherever I was. My laptop went everywhere with me, and when smartphones started coming out, I got a BlackBerry (I have since moved on to an iPhone). I could check voicemail and return calls and respond to e-mails. I even set up a system whereby I could access my office computer remotely.

I truly believed I could work from anywhere.

> *If the COVID-19 pandemic has taught us anything, it's the importance of being able to work from anywhere.*

But when the pandemic hit, I found out how wrong I'd been! If I was forced to work from home, there were several important things I still couldn't do. Not good! I could still access my office computer remotely, but it was a bit awkward and clunky,

So What Do I Use?

Since this book is, in great measure, about how I do things, at least by way of example, I will tell you what I use and why. You can then draw your own conclusions (and comparisons) in deciding what to do in your firm.

As I was heavily into Word and Excel, and despite the fact that I am an Apple shop, I opted for Microsoft 365 (formerly Office 365). However, that was not the only reason I did so. This platform does far more than provide the latest versions of all their software and store their files in a secure, encrypted cloud; it has a whole host of other applications that integrate with one another, including a scheduling app (Bookings), Outlook for calendar and e-mail (which also integrates tightly with my MS Exchange account), and Teams for collaboration with my virtual assistant. There is also the automation platform Power Automate that I discussed in a previous section. That provided a powerful automation option guaranteed to work with all of their tools and workflows.

This catalog of apps was key to my decision, as otherwise I would have had to put together my own hodgepodge of separate platforms (often at separate costs for each) in order to get the same benefit. For example, if I had decided on Google Workspace, I would have had to get a collaboration platform like Slack, a scheduling app like Calendly or Tidycal, a planning platform like Trello, and be limited to Zapier for automation. As you will see below, how all of your cloud platforms integrate with each other is a key factor in a virtual law firm.

Your Phone System

Part of practicing from anywhere is being reachable anywhere. This is certainly true of e-mail, but what about phone calls? If you aren't at your office desk to pick up the ringing handset, what do you do? You could set up call forwarding to send all calls to your cell phone, but what about outgoing calls (assuming you don't want people to have your cell phone number by getting it from caller ID)? Also, you must remember to turn off the forwarding when you get to the office. Clearly, your phone system must be virtual as well.

This means getting a VoIP (Voice Over Internet Protocol) system. I did this a couple of years ago, partly to get away from the high prices of the traditional phone company, but also to make it easier to work from anywhere. There are several vendors out there, including RingCentral, Nextiva, Vonage, GoToConnect, and DialPad. Which one you choose is up to you, but you should be sure to get at least the following features from the service.

A PBX Equivalent. If you've ever had one of these, you know what I'm talking about! If you have staff, you need to have a main line and (depending on your call volume) one or two "hunt lines" for calls to roll over to if the main line is busy. It should also have "extensions," or unique numbers for each member of your staff. These lines can either ring through to a VoIP-capable desk handset or to that person's computer for calls on a headset. Each should have a separate voicemail box with the ability to e-mail the voicemail message to the user. If you still have a PBX, a VoIP system will provide considerable savings.

Free Fax Line. You will have incoming and outgoing faxes. All you should have to do is use the vendor's software to type in a fax number, attach a cover sheet (if needed), and select one or more PDFs to send out. Receiving faxes is also easy! You should just get an alert on their software (on your computer and your phone/tablet) and view/save to cloud drive the PDF that is the "fax." You never have to touch paper again to fax something! I can just pull out my phone, wherever I am, and view an incoming fax to see if it needs immediate action!

Clearly, your phone system must be virtual as well. This means getting a VoIP (Voice Over Internet Protocol) system.

Make Your Cell Phone Your Office Phone. Their software should also reside on your cell phone, allowing you to make outgoing calls without revealing your cell phone number; it will just spoof your office number! By doing this you can make calls from anywhere comfortably.

Texting. I am not a big believer in texting for case-related communication because there is usually no way of preserving those texts with the case file. However, some clients prefer texting for some types of communication, and routine stuff (like a note to you that traffic is heavy, and they will be 10 minutes late to their appointment) can be communicated easily without giving the person your cell phone number!

Having these features means that you don't have to mess with call forwarding. Calls can come through on your computer (or headset) or ring to the vendor's software on your smartphone, so you can receive calls from anywhere. Having a VoIP system has saved me money and allowed to kick my service and availability up a notch!

Your Payment & Retention System

Getting retained and paid can be much easier in the virtual world! I have found that to be true, and I firmly believe that I have gotten more clients and made more money by accepting credit cards. This is not possible in all areas of my practice (particularly bankruptcy), but it has been a boon to my traffic court, DUI, and collection defense practice. There are many clients I have not ever met with face to face, other than through Zoom or Microsoft Teams.

Yes, taking credit cards means that the issuing bank gets a piece of your action (close to 3%), but the increased revenues you will see from doing it will far outweigh it! Also, people tend to spend more when they can put it on their card, because to them it isn't really coming out of their pocket, especially if they don't pay their balances off every month. The bank is financing your fee for them!

Again, you can use whatever vendor you like, but I would like to put in a good word for LawPay, which is the one I use. There are three key reasons for this:

- Their fees are very low (1.9% at the time of this writing), and if the client is using a debit card, they just charge a $2 processing fee. How cool is that?

- They do not take their fee out at the time of the transaction; they bill you monthly by ACH from your bank account.

- It integrates with Clio, so I can send bills and receive payment through their platform, and LawPay waives monthly fees.

No matter what, the most important thing is to be able to accept credit or debit cards. Sending a payment link is easy, processing payments through your accounting system (I use QuickBooks) is simpler because they charge separately for their fees, and I get paid faster!

The other part of this system is the retainer agreement. Being virtual means that clients shouldn't have to be in your office to sign on the dotted line. For me, I use DocuSign because it integrates through Clio and makes it much easier to get retainer agreements out the door and signed faster. The PDF of the executed agreement can then be saved to my cloud drive along with all the other case-related documents.

Paperless Office Workflows

If you truly want to have a virtual law firm, then you must go paperless. Physical documents must have homes in the real world, and as such, can't be accessed from anywhere. This means that, other than the need to maintain certain types of physical documents to be in compliance with certain court rules, nothing in your practice should be on paper. This may seem a bit extreme, but once you get a system in place, you will wonder why you didn't do it sooner.

end, in handling the typical matter. That will give you a good idea of the steps you'll need to take, and the tools you will need to have, to accomplish this.

Outgoing Documents and Correspondence

All outgoing correspondence is scanned before it goes out, including enclosures, and I don't bother to print a copy for a file. Documents I create in Word or Excel I convert to PDF to send to the client, the court, or opposing counsel. The Mac has a great "print to PDF" feature that I use every day. Things seldom get printed to paper anymore. Make sure that the software you have has the ability to create a PDF version of any document you create. Word and Excel have the ability to "Save As" a PDF document. Look for it under the File menu.

Incoming Documents and Correspondence

All incoming paper correspondence and documents get scanned. There are some firms that will then shred the originals, but I will sometimes retain them, depending on the type of matter they are for. I must admit, though, that the amount of paper that comes into my office through the mail that needs to be retained at all has been diminishing. In most instances my client or adversary will send me a PDF by e-mail, or a fax, and I won't need to scan and shred.

Note Taking and Document Review

But there are times when you want to put pen to paper. For example, when I get discovery in from the police on a traffic court matter or DUI, I need to review it and make notes. I first take the PDFs of the documents and put it on the folder I access from my iPad. I then bring it up on its screen and, using an app called Peiperl and my Apple Pencil, I highlight and underline sections and jot notes in the margin! The documents, with annotations, are still accessible from my computer or any other device tied to that cloud storage. In other words, I don't need to look at it on my tablet to review my notes! Even if you have a Windows PC, you should be able to do the same thing utilizing this Apple hardware, because the marked-up document can still reside (and be viewed) on your PC.

I also use my iPad and Apple Pencil to take notes during client meetings or initial consultations with potential clients. PDFExpert allows me to create blank PDFs with white, yellow or blue pages that are either blank, lined, or have a grid. I use yellow lined pages because they most resemble a legal pad. For bankruptcies I have a standard interview form that I fill out. With a couple of taps, I can make a copy of the form, fill it out, and rename it with the name of the potential client. Then, if they retain me and I open a file, I can move the document into the folder on the cloud drive for that file!

Let's say your associate or paralegal prepares a document for you on his or her computer, like a will or a deed, and then sends the PDF to you to review it. Imagine just pulling it up on your tablet, marking it up like you would with a pen and paper, and then zapping it back to that person for revisions based on your changes and comments! The whole thing can be accomplished without producing a single sheet of paper!

Help Is Available!

As you can see, moving to the cloud, being virtual, paperless, and able to work from anywhere is liberating and, more importantly, economical! With employees that can work from home, you can save on space (which saves on rent). If you already have more space than you need, you can downsize once your lease is up for renewal (or rent out some of it if you own your building). Paper-based overhead can be eliminated, and you can provide better service to your clients!

But at the same time, it all seems rather intimidating. Who has the time to do the research and implement the solutions and platforms that are right for your practice? If you have decided to move your practice to the cloud, become virtual, and switch to paperless, but realize that you don't have the time or the expertise to do it yourself, then I can help! Just reach out to me through www.StevenJRichardson.com to schedule a no-obligation call and take your first step towards a better way to practice law!

Afterword

expectations. You owe it to yourself to reach out to them for free website analysis at www.FWMAnalysis.com.

So what's next? Where do you go from here? Well, as I said at the beginning of the book, the first thing you need to do is regain control of your time. Banish the time bandits, wrangle the telephone into submission, and get better focus on what you need to do each day, and how much time it will take to do it. It is only then that you will be able to achieve the focus necessary to gain clarity on the purpose for your practice, its most important values, and its mission in delivering legal services.

Once you have completed your "meta level thinking" to see the big picture, you can move on to the strategies and systems that you need to put into place to allow you to: delegate the tasks that you shouldn't be doing (or do not require an attorney to do), and know that those tasks will be completed properly, consistently, and with the high level of quality that you want. You will then have a scalable business that will expand much more easily, while making you more money and not demanding more of your time.

I know, it is a very challenging thing to undertake, and you may not think it is possible. You may not think that you have the skill sets necessary to achieve all the different elements to make the enterprise a success. The most important thing to bear in mind, though, is that you are not alone in taking this journey. As I have said throughout this book, I have already taken this journey and would be happy to help you along this path and maximize your chances of success.

Just check out the programs, webinars, strategic partners, and workshops at www.StevenJRichardson.com to find out what

I can do for you. I also have resources to make available to you to help you implement the system. Check them out at the back of this book. They can provide you with additional information on time management, time blocking, automation, and the implementation of systems in your firm.

The longest journey starts with a single step; all you have to do is take it!

Resources

RocketMatter (www.RocketMatter.com)

FileVine (www.FileVine.com)

Practice Panther (www.PracticePanther.com)

Zapier (www.Zapier.com)

Keyboard Maestro (www.KeyboardMaestro.com)

Hazel (www.Noodlesoft.com)

TextExpander (www.TextExpander.com)

David Sparks Field Guides (learn.macsparky.com)

TubeBuddy (www.TubeBuddy.com)

RingCentral (www.RingCentral.com)

Nextiva (www.Nextiva.com)

Vonage (www.Vonage.com)

GoToConnect (www.GoTo.com)

DialPad (www.DialPad.com)

LawPay (www.LawPay.com)

DocuSign (www.DocuSign.com)

Adobe (www.adobe.com)

Nuance (www.Nuance.com)

PDFExpert (www.PDFExpert.com)

OmniFocus (www.www.omnigroup.com/omnifocus)

Things (www.culturedcode.com/things)

Todoist (www.Todoist.com)

Companies

Foster Web Marketing (www.FosterWebMarketing.com)

The Video Marketing School (www.thevideomarketingschool.com)

Ruby Receptionists (www.Ruby.com)

Absolute Marketing (www.GetAbsoluteMarketing.com)

Fujitsu (www.fujitsu.com/us/products/computing/peripheral/scanners/soho/)

Made in the USA
Monee, IL
04 November 2026

67381815R10105